YOUTILITY

why **SMART MARKETING**
is about **HELP** *not* **HYPE**

YOUTILITY

JAY BAER

PORTFOLIO / PENGUIN

PORTFOLIO / PENGUIN
Published by the Penguin Group
Penguin Group (USA) Inc., 375 Hudson Street,
New York, New York 10014, USA

USA | Canada | UK | Ireland | Australia | New Zealand | India | South Africa | China
Penguin Books Ltd, Registered Offices: 80 Strand, London WC2R 0RL, England
For more information about the Penguin Group visit penguin.com

Illustration credits
Page 53: From the book ZMOT. By permission of Google Inc.
Pages 104 and 145: By permission of Marketoonist LLC

ISBN 978-1-59184-666-6

Printed in the United States of America
10 9 8 7 6 5 4 3 2 1

Set in Sabon LT Std
Designed by Elyse Strongin, Neuwirth & Associates, Inc.

For my brother Jeff,
who was so useful I used to pay him to fix my bike.

CONTENTS

FOREWORD

I was officially scared to death. It was November 2008. The stock market was in a terrible nose dive. Presidential candidates John McCain and Barack Obama debated what should be done about failing banks and financial institutions. To say the U.S. economy was in a tailspin would be an understatement, and consumer confidence was suddenly, almost overnight, shaken to the core.

Within days of the market collapse I had four customers withdraw their deposits. More would follow in the coming weeks. What had appeared to be a healthy late spring and winter for my business was becoming a nightmare.

I was a "pool guy," as homeowners often call us. Along with my two business partners I had owned River Pools and Spas in Warsaw, Virginia, since 2001. We started with a beat-up pickup truck, three guys, and a dream. By 2008 we had become a formidable in-ground swimming pool construction company with more than seventy fiberglass pool installations a year in Virginia and Maryland.

Going into 2008 I was oozing with confidence. Our brand was expanding, and we were pushing growth as hard as we possibly could. Finally, after years of physical, mental, and emotional sacrifice we were going to experience the fruits of our labors. But no amount of sacrifice or experience could have prepared us for the economic collapse. The faucet that had been flowing wide open during the previous decade suddenly refused to allow even a drop to fall.

By January 2009, our company was on the brink of complete financial ruin. The phone simply wasn't ringing. It stood to reason; one thing consumers rarely do in the worst economic times since the 1930s is sit around the dinner table and decide to purchase a swimming pool. Even in the rare circumstances when there were interested customers, banks had made luxury-lending nearly impossible with the tightening of credit and the evaporation of home equity due to the collapse of the real estate market. We had almost no projects for the foreseeable future. Our credit lines were maxed out, our sixteen employees were sitting at home with nothing to do, and our bank accounts were overdrawn for three consecutive weeks.

I was depressed, scared, and out of ideas. I found myself turning to the one place we seem to go to find the answers we're looking for—the Internet. Since I certainly wasn't installing pools, I had plenty of time to research new marketing and business concepts; as I did, concepts like "blogging," "inbound marketing," "content marketing," and "social media" kept coming up again and again and again.

Like most of us I had an inherent sense that business and marketing were shifting to the web, but, as a not particularly computer-savvy guy, it wasn't something that had ever seemed applicable to *my* business. But, I'd never been more ready to try something new. Unless we figured out a way to generate more leads and sales without spending money on advertising, we were going to close our doors, and my business partners and I would lose our homes.

It was time to sink or swim.

What I discovered first, and what will become exceptionally clear in this book, is that consumers of all types expect
to find answers on the Internet now, and companies that can
best provide that information garner trust and sales and loyalty. Success flows to organizations that inform, not organizations that promote. It's a fundamental change in how I
think about business, and you'll think differently, too, after
reading *Youtility*.

My new plan for River Pools and Spas was simple: I decided to act like a swimming pool consumer instead of a swimming pool installer. I applied this methodology in two ways
that changed my company and my life.

First, I brainstormed every single question I'd ever received
from a prospect or customer. Since I had been selling swimming pools for about eight years at the time, this list quickly
grew to hundreds of questions. Then I answered every single
one of those questions with its own blog post, adding hundreds
of new pages to my website (www.riverpoolsandspas.com) in
the process. I'd already answered these questions face-to-face,
on the telephone, and through e-mail, so I knew the answers;
I'd just never considered putting them on a blog.

It wasn't easy. I wasn't much of a writer, and I was already
working sixty or more hours a week doing whatever I could
to keep our company alive. But, late at night, when my wife
and four young kids were asleep, I'd sit at the kitchen table
and write. Each post took about an hour, and, unlike most
companies that think the word "blog" means "brag," I never
made the articles a River Pools advertisement. Instead, I simply answered the questions as honestly and frankly as I could.

I added new posts to the website every week, and it became immediately obvious that they were having an impact

on my business. We were getting more website visitors, mostly because Google was providing links to the new posts when consumers searched for information about the same issues I was addressing. This increase in traffic also generated significant new leads, connecting River Pools and Spas to potential customers who otherwise might never have known about us. The website, never a big part of our business, suddenly became central to our operations.

I also started getting comments from prospects who took the time to write little notes in the "contact us" form on the site:

"I love your website, Marcus, it's so informative, I spent over an hour on there the other night!"

"Marcus, thank you for answering all of our questions, we can't tell you how much easier you've made this process!"

"Marcus, everywhere I look online for information about fiberglass pools I keep seeing your name!!"

I had started the magical journey toward Youtility.

For years, sales appointments had been arduous for me. I would arrive at customers' homes and find their knowledge about pools (types, costs, accessories, etc.) so poor that I'd literally have to spend hours with them at their kitchen tables, teaching them all of this basic information, just to get to a point where we could start talking about what it was they wanted and how much it was all going to cost. But now the website had become a useful resource for these prospects, and I was finding many homeowners were incredibly informed *before* I ever even set foot in their homes. They were engaging in self-serve information before ever contacting us, a massive shift in consumer behavior that is illustrated and illuminated in this book.

Educated consumers are sometimes threatening to salespeople. Do car salesmen want their prospective buyers to know exactly how much the dealership paid for the car? Do airlines want customers to be alerted when fares go down? There's no question that information changes the balance of power, but I found this to be a tremendous benefit, not a hindrance. Each time I encountered a prospective pool-buying family who had educated themselves on our website (and other sources) before I met them, the length of the sales appointment would decrease, and the likelihood of turning that prospect into a customer went up.

I decided to look deeper into this situation, and, at the beginning of 2011, I analyzed behavior patterns on our website in hopes of better understanding why some visitors fill out a contact form on the site but never advance past that point, while others eventually become customers. As I compared these two groups of site visitors, one number jumped out at me . . . thirty. It was the tipping point. If a visitor to our website reads at least thirty pages of our information *before* we go on an in-home sales appointment, they buy a pool 80 percent of the time. Considering the industry closing rate average is around 10 percent, this was a shocking revelation. They weren't just self-educating, they were self-qualifying, too. By the time they contacted us for an in-person appointment, they were predisposed to working with us.

As you'll see in *Youtility*, consumers' desire to consume inherently useful information has never been greater. In 2012 the average new River Pools and Spas customer who filled out a form on the website and eventually bought a swimming pool read 105 pages of our site. When we started this journey, the entire website was just 20 pages. Today, we offer more than 850 pages of information, with more added all the time.

In a time when swimming pool companies all over the United States were going out of business, we managed to grow our market share, with more than 80 percent of all our sales coming directly from the Internet. In 2007, when the economy was going great and pool sales were easy, we spent about $250,000 in advertising to achieve roughly $4 million in sales.

In 2011, when the economy was a mess and luxury spending was in the dumps, we spent $20,000 in advertising to generate $4.5 million in sales. What changed? We became a Youtility, not just a swimming pool company.

Today, despite the fact that we're just a little swimming pool company in Virginia, we have the most trafficked swimming pool website in the world. Five years ago, if you had asked me and my business partners what we do, the answer would have been simple: "We build in-ground fiberglass swimming pools." Now we say: "We are the best teachers in the world on the subject of fiberglass swimming pools, and we happen to build them as well."

This Book Is About You

People often tell me the River Pools and Spas story couldn't have been done in other industries and niches. But nothing could be further from the truth. As you'll discover in this book, Youtility works in just about every industry; in big companies and small companies, in exciting companies and less exciting companies, in companies that embrace technology and those that do not, in new companies and companies that are more than 150 years old.

You and your company absolutely can succeed using these principles. You just have to fundamentally change the way you think about marketing, its role, and the relationship it creates with your customers and prospects.

Because River Pools and Spas is on solid ground these days, I've left the day-to-day operations of the company in the hands of my two business partners and now run my own marketing company and brand . . . The Sales Lion. I've replicated the process and have a website (www.thesaleslion.com) where I answer marketing questions the same way I used to answer swimming pool questions. I travel around the country working with companies to show them how to sell more by selling less.

You will do this eventually. Whether you read this book and get started right away, or take a few more years to put this concept into practice in your company, someday you'll embrace marketing that is truly useful. Because this isn't just a good idea or a counterintuitive way to communicate— it's a reaction to huge changes in how consumers behave, what they expect, and whom they trust. This is why I was so thrilled to have the opportunity to write the foreword to this book. As someone who has poured my heart and soul into helping businesses understand the ideas and execute the strategies I have found so useful, I've come to appreciate the few in this realm who match my passion and enthusiasm for this new way of doing business. Without question, Jay Baer is one of those people.

In fact, when he told me the title to this book—*Youtility*—my mind nearly exploded with excitement. Somehow he managed to perfectly put into one word everything River Pools had become and everything I hope other businesses will strive to be.

When it comes down to it, my friends, this book isn't about changing your marketing, it's about changing your mindset. I did it. Now it's your turn.

MARCUS SHERIDAN
"The Sales Lion" and co-owner of River Pools and Spas

YOUTILITY

INTRODUCTION

Make a Customer Today, or Create a Customer for Life

"**L**et me get this straight. You're in the business of fixing stuff for money, but you have dozens of videos that show people how to fix things themselves? How does that make business sense?"

In 2009 at the La Quinta Resort in La Quinta, California, an audience member asked this question of Robert Stephens, founder of the computer- and electronics-services company Geek Squad. Stephens had just concluded a keynote presentation to the Counselor's Academy section of the Public Relations Society of America (PRSA), showing attendees the Geek Squad HQ YouTube channel (ar.gy/geeksquad), home to more than two hundred videos on subjects ranging from spyware removal to the nuances of Microsoft's new Windows 8 operating system.

Stephens's answer forever changed how I think about marketing. "Well, the reality is that our best customers are the people that think they can do it themselves," he said. "And the other thing you have to realize is that eventually everybody is going to be out of their depth. They won't be able to do it themselves, and at that point whom are they going to call? Somebody randomly out of a phone book, or are they going to call Geek Squad, whose videos they've been watching over and over for six, eight, ten, twelve minutes with our logo in the corner?"

Starting as the sole employee with $200 of working capital in 1994, Stephens ultimately sold Geek Squad to retail giant Best Buy in 2006, where the scope and scale of Geek Squad exploded. In 2007 alone, twelve thousand Geek Squad agents generated an estimated $280 million of profit on $1 billion in revenue.[1] What Stephens understood earlier than most marketers is that simultaneous shifts in how and why customers consume information have fundamentally altered the success formula for modern business. You can't survive by shouting the loudest and relying solely on anachronistic interruption marketing. You can't proclaim you're featuring the "biggest sale ever!" every day. You can't simply rewrite a portion of your online brochure and hope that Google funnels customers to your website.

Today's consumers are staring at an invitation avalanche, with every company asking for likes, follows, clicks and attention. This is on top of all the legacy advertising that envelops us like a straitjacket. There are only two ways for companies to break through in an environment that is unprecedented in its competitiveness and cacophony. They can be "amazing" or they can be useful. Lots of books have been written—one of them by me—that tell you how to be an amazing company. Pretty much all of them say you can win hearts and minds by doing things differently, providing knock-your-socks-off customer service, or fundamentally changing your corporate culture.

While being amazing can work, it's difficult to do and doesn't produce reliable, linear results. So instead of betting all your money on "amazing," what if you instead relied on a simple, universal method of marketing and business success—one that's never been more important or easier to accomplish? It's the same method Robert Stephens mastered with the Geek Squad video program.

What if instead of trying to be amazing you just focused on being useful? What if you decided to inform, rather than promote? You know that expression "If you give a man a fish, you feed him for a day; if you teach a man to fish, you feed him for a lifetime"? Well, the same is true for marketing: If you sell something, you make a customer today; if you help someone, you make a customer for life.

I call this Youtility. Not "utility," because a utility is a faceless commodity. Youtility is marketing upside down. Instead of marketing that's needed by companies, Youtility is marketing that's wanted by customers. Youtility is massively useful information, provided for free, that creates long-term trust and kinship between your company and your customers.

The difference between helping and selling is just two letters. But those two letters now make all the difference.

The way customers gather information about companies and make purchase decisions has changed. Consumers' time and attention has never been more scarce, and their suspicion of lazy interruption marketing has never been more acute. In this climate, Youtility is not an option; it's necessary.

In this book, I'll explore the three types of historical consumer-awareness strategies, including the new one that supports Youtility, and explain the three facts of Youtility marketing. I'll also describe the six-step process you can use to build Youtility in your business. Throughout, I'll show you examples of more than twenty companies, of all sizes and categories, that are successfully using this framework to build profitable and long-lasting relationships with customers.

Let's go.

PART I
Turning Marketing Upside Down

CHAPTER 1
Top-of-Mind Awareness

Throughout history we've embraced three categories of marketing. The first is top-of-mind awareness. I suspect you've heard of it. The idea is that you need to have a sustained level of marketing and messaging, so when the customer is ready to buy, they think of your product first. Achieving and maintaining top-of-mind awareness requires substantial ongoing advertising spending, which means it generally only works well for already-popular brands.

This approach hasn't changed much for eons. Since the first caveman sold a rock to another caveman, marketers have been sending messages out into the marketplace, saying, "We've got great stuff. Buy it."

As Avinash Kaushik, coauthor of *Web Analytics 2.0* and *Web Analytics: An Hour a Day*, says, "We've never managed to get beyond a medium that allowed us to just shout; so TV, magazines, radio, newspapers are all wonderful channels, but are essentially dumb in the sense that you put something out there and pray that the people who are in market at the moment will consume content on the channels, and see your advertising, and be so wowed by it that they will run to the store and buy your product."[1]

Top-of-mind awareness isn't inherently flawed, but it isn't very surgical, and it hasn't evolved much despite changing technologies. Even with so many new tools with which to convey our messages to prospective customers, especially social media like Facebook, Twitter, and beyond, few businesses are actually doing anything markedly different than they used to. Facebook is a fancy photo scrapbook for many businesses. Twitter is often just a tiny press-release machine.

Here is an example from a music producer on Twitter whose handle is "I Make Hit Beats." He is @5StarBeats4Sale. Here's a tweet from him in all caps, which is a nice touch.

I MAKE HIT BEATS @5StarBeats4Sale   7m
CHECK OUT MY HIGH QUALITY BEATS ON SALE AT $10 BUY 1 GET 3 FREE (BEAT PACK) VISIT MY SITE NOW AT 5STARBEATZ.COM , THANKS!!!!!!!!
Expand

I MAKE HIT BEATS @5StarBeats4Sale   8m
HIGH DEF QUALITY BEATS ON SALE AT 5STARBEATZ.COM GO NOW AND DON'T MISS OUT ON GREAT DEALS LIKE BUY 1 GET 3 FREE $10 BANGERS!
Expand

I MAKE HIT BEATS @5StarBeats4Sale   9m
CHECK OUT MY NEW HIGH QUALITY BEATS JUST UPLOADED....BUY 1 GET 3 FREE $10, LIMITEF TIME VALUE AT 5STARBEATZ.COM!!!!!!!!!!!!!!!!!!!!!
Expand

If you look into his history, you'll find that Mister 5starbeatz. com often spews several tweets in a row within seven or eight minutes that are fundamentally the same all-caps message. What we have here is not new marketing. It's not a new way to communicate to customers. It's the old way, just via 140 characters at a time. It's the same shouting with a different megaphone.

Whether it relies on old media or new, top-of-mind awareness is less effective than ever as a marketing strategy for two reasons: You can't promote to people you can't find, and distrust of business erodes its foundation.

You Can't Promote to People You Can't Find: The Fracturing of the Media Landscape

At its core, top-of-mind awareness relies on the ability to reach large numbers of potential consumers efficiently. Doing so used to be a relatively straightforward scheme. When Americans had just three major television networks, it was easy to reach large swaths of potential buyers with a single commercial. When overwhelming majorities of American households subscribed to the local newspaper and tuned into local radio stations, businesses with even very small trade areas could reach the majority of their prospective customers with a few, targeted media purchases.

Those days are over.

In 1977, the number one television show in the United States was *Happy Days*. In 1977 *Happy Days* did a 31.5 rating, meaning that 31.5 percent of Americans living in a household with a television watched the program.

Ten years later, in 1987, the number one show was *The*

Cosby Show, which did a 27.8 rating. Ten years after that, the number one show was *Seinfeld*. It did a 21.7 rating. And ten years later, the number one show was *American Idol*, which did a 16.1 rating.

In 2011, for the first time, the number one show wasn't really a show at all. *Sunday Night Football* did a seasonal average 12.9 rating as the number one television program in America.

So, from 1977 to 2011, the number one TV show, generating the biggest audience in the country, went from a 31.5 rating to a 12.9 rating.[2] The number of Americans (and the number of Americans in a household with a television) has of course increased during the same period, so a 12.9 rating today represents more viewers than a 12.9 in 1977, but this isn't about total viewers. In fact, Americans are watching more television than ever, although often now as part of a dual-screen environment, complete with tablet computer on the lap.

What's far more important is that the number one program is being watched by fewer than 13 percent of the nation. The fragmentation of the media landscape in the past twenty years is remarkable. In the era of just three main television networks, buying advertising time wasn't a particularly difficult task. Now, one of the toughest jobs in the world—and most certainly one of the most difficult and thankless in marketing—is media buying, because there are countless ways to reach audiences. But there's no place where you can reach everybody, not like you used to be able to, which makes top-of-mind awareness much more difficult as a marketing approach.

The decline of the American newspaper industry is accelerating, with century-old publications partially or wholly giving up on ink and paper, trying to cling to the life preserver of online-only distribution. According to the Pew Internet Center, 2011 advertising revenue for American newspapers was less than half of what it was in 2006.[3] Certainly, the economics of chopping down trees and delivering a physical product to subscribers' doorsteps each morning is a bit dubious at present. But the greater threat affecting newspapers (and in some cases, magazines) is that they've lost their special role as a trusted, current source of information.

I still subscribe to a local newspaper. I'm a member of Generation X, which didn't grow up with virtual media and mobile technology, but adapted to it—usually in the workplace first, and then personally. So while my kids think it's an anachronism on the scale of churning our own butter to have a newspaper delivered, I have never known a day without one. But it most assuredly takes me a lot less time to scan the paper each morning, given that I have already read the national, international, and sports news the night before on a mobile device.

When people want to know what's going on, or want to tap in to the zeitgeist of the moment, they don't wait for the next morning's newspaper. They look online, and especially at Twitter, which has become the news ticker of the modern age. Twitter's power and popularity doesn't stem from its usage. In fact, 8 percent of Americans twelve or older have an account, according to 2012 data from Edison Research.[4] But awareness of the service is almost universal and is on par with Facebook, which has eight or nine times more users in the United States. The power and popularity of Twitter stem from those who use it (celebrities and thought leaders) and from the curious fact that traditional media constantly report on tweets, using them interchangeably with direct quotations.

The throats of print media are being cut not just by Twitter's ascendant role as a real-time information source, but by the almost comical proliferation of blogs. According to Nielsen's NM Incite research, there were more than 173 million blogs in late 2011.[5]

Unofficially, about half of those 173 million blogs are about cats, somewhat blunting their impact as a news source. But those non-cat blogs are taking readers away from print media. Meanwhile, new technologies like DVR, satellite radio, and ad blocking have made it easy for consumers to ignore your sales pitch. Social media, which have been em-

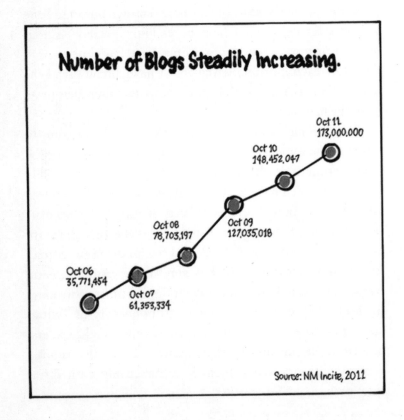

Number of Blogs Steadily Increasing.

Oct 11
173,000,000

Oct 10
148,452,047

Oct 09
127,035,018

Oct 08
78,703,197

Oct 07
61,353,334

Oct 06
35,771,454

Source: NM Incite, 2011

braced by brands for their ability to better target audiences, also give those audiences even more opportunities to look the other way when you start marketing to them.

A 2011 research project called "The Social Breakup" from interactive marketing firm ExactTarget found that 55 percent of Facebook users in the United States have "liked" a brand on Facebook, and then later decided they didn't want to see that company's posts.[6] ExactTarget describes consumers' ability to unilaterally fray or sever the top-of-mind awareness relationship this way:

> Communication practices that convey warmth and respect for the consumer through one channel can just as easily convey indifference—or desperation—through another. If the company fails any of these relationship tests, a "social breakup"—i.e., an "unsubscribe," "unfan," "unlike," or "unfollow"—is all but inevitable. When the consumer is no longer happy in the relationship, they will actively break off contact with the company . . . or just ignore their communications in the hopes the company will get the message that it's over.

Top-of-mind awareness requires companies to send messages consistently, but today's consumers are besieged with every company of every type, size, and description jostling for attention, making pleas to friend, follow, subscribe, read, watch, and click. Unimaginative marketers attempt to stand out with message frequency, or by exchanging bribes for attention (resulting in an explosion of Facebook contests and giveaways, among other tactics).

But sending messages too often can have unintended consequences. ExactTarget's 2012 United Kingdom version of

"The Social Breakup" study found that the most often cited reason consumers "unlike" a company on Facebook is that they felt "bombarded by messages."[7] And, as noted by Jeff Rohrs, ExactTarget's vice president of Marketing Research and Education, all consumers "have to do is just ignore the messages over a period of time, and they slowly get suppressed by Facebook. You simply won't show up anymore, even if your brand is still technically "liked.""

Distrust Chips Away at Top-of-Mind Awareness

The other reason top-of-mind awareness is in peril as a marketing tactic is that many consumers don't trust businesses. Each year since 2000, the global public relations consultancy Edelman conducts a comprehensive survey that investigates which institutions are trusted and distrusted worldwide. In 2013, this "Edelman Trust Barometer" found businesses were trusted by 58 percent of survey respondents globally.[8] This is up from 53 percent in 2012. Put in a somewhat more strident context, this means that for every ten of the potential customers you're trying to reach with your messages, more than four don't trust you.

This lack of trust in businesses has been an issue for at least a decade. In the United States, 44 percent trusted business in 2001, and 45 percent in 2012. In other major economies that have marketing mechanics similar to America's, the data is even more frightening, with the United Kingdom, France, and Germany trusting businesses at a 32 percent rate in 2001, and 31 percent in 2012.

If half of your potential customers (at best) are distrustful of your business, that's a problem. Because trust matters. A

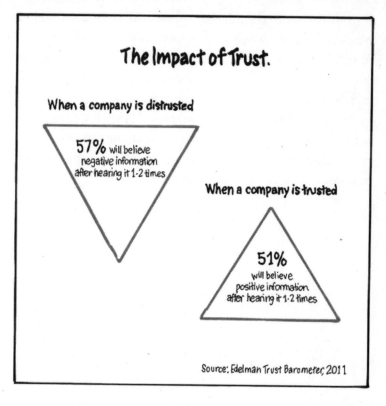

lot. Edelman finds that when a company is distrusted, 57 percent of people will believe negative information after hearing it just one or two times. Conversely, when companies are trusted, 51 percent of people believe positive information about the company after hearing it just one or two times.

"Trust has never been more important as a corporate asset, and it needs to be managed for people to believe the information you're putting out," says Amy Treanor, executive vice president of Edelman Square, the division of the firm responsible for the Trust Barometer.[9]

Companies of all sizes and types can and should take steps to buttress their trustworthiness, and in the most recent version of the research, Edelman published "The Six Building Blocks of Trust" to help clarify how trust can be built. They found that what might be considered the base elements of trust, such as financial performance and accountability, are merely table stakes in a much more nuanced game.

"To really be a trusted enterprise," Treanor says, "you need to focus on the more societal and engagement activities: transparency, employee engagement, listening to your customers, and putting them ahead of profits."

CHAPTER 2
Frame-of-Mind Awareness

The second type of marketing we've embraced doesn't have the history of top-of-mind awareness, but it certainly has the hype. This is frame-of-mind awareness, and it is based on the strategy of reaching potential customers when they are in an active shopping and buying mode. The idea is that stepping in front of consumers' inquisition train at precisely the moment they need your product or service leads to colossal business impacts.

The strategy dates to the 1880s. The perhaps-too-convenient legend holds that in 1883 a Wyoming printer ran out of white paper and used yellow instead,[1] inadvertently spawning the global, multi-billion dollar telephone directory industry. A more reliable genesis is Reuben H. Donnelley's production of the first Yellow Pages in 1886.[2] After that, it was off to the races, with Yellow Pages circa 1990 being as close to a marketing must-do as has ever existed.

The disintermediation of the Yellow Pages by the World Wide Web is well documented. Even sloppily executed searches of Twitter can locate ironic photographs and pithy guffaws every time a printed directory is dropped off at the home of a digerati. The invention of the visual browser was the first shot across the bow of the Yellow Pages. But when Yahoo! became the first popularized web directory in 1994 and 1995,[3] relying on a cabal of young techies to categorize websites by hand, it didn't seem all that impressive. At least it didn't to me,[4] and I was working in what passed for the web industry back then. But once Excite, Alta Vista, and the new breed of fully computerized search and retrieval software commenced (culminating with Google's introduction in 1999), the economies of speed and scale won out. Not to mention the relative ease of being able to carry a conduit to most of the world's information in your pocket via smartphone versus opening an eight-pound book to find only phone numbers within twenty miles of your home.

The Rise of Inbound Marketing and Why It's Half the Story

In recent years, the process of creating text, audio, video, and other online assets, and optimizing them to appear when prospective customers are ready to pull the trigger on a purchase has been coined "Inbound Marketing." HubSpot (hubspot.com), a software company that licenses technology to enable midsized companies to execute the tactics of this strategy, created the "Inbound Marketing" term in 2006.

"We got the inspiration for the company from [cofounder] Dharmesh [Shah]'s blog," says Brian Halligan, HubSpot cofounder and coauthor of *Inbound Marketing: Get Found Using Google, Social Media, and Blogs*. "He's got this blog, onstartups.com, and he'd do great with it. He had tons of links in to it from other sites, and any kind of cultural article he wrote would take off on Digg and reddit. We just grew very, very interested in that, and juxtaposed it with the way, frankly, that I'd always done marketing. I thought 'this is a much better way to do it.'"

Mission accomplished, Brian. The 2012 HubSpot customer event (called, unsurprisingly, Inbound Conference) attracted more than 2,800 disciples, and the number of times "inbound marketing" is searched on Google has increased roughly twenty-fold since 2007.[5]

Inbound marketing is a powerful tool. I've spent sizable chunks of my own career helping companies improve in this arena, which is why I know that the power of frame-of-mind awareness isn't absolute. There are more than a few companies that believe findability is the sole fulcrum of success, and it simply isn't true because frame-of-mind awareness doesn't create demand. It cannot. It simply fulfills demand that already exists.

I don't know much about you, other than your evident interest in improving your business (and your discerning taste in books). But I know for certain there's one thing you don't do. You do not go to Google and say, "I'm in the market to buy something. I'm not sure what. Anything, really. Just surprise me."

By definition (and even by name), searching is a very specific, self-directed behavior. You need something, you go get it. You don't introduce products and concepts and categories while searching, using frame-of-mind awareness. It's not a browsable medium that you're going to curl up with on a bearskin rug in front of a cozy fire. It's wham, bam, thanks for the link, ma'am. Small businesses, in particular, are often guilty of over-reliance on search marketing to drive inquiries and sales. As marketing author Seth Godin writes in his blog, "Most small businesses believe that they're too small to have an impact on the whole market, so they resort to picking the fruit that's already grown instead of planting their own seeds. It's far easier to wait until someone is ready to buy than it is to persuade them to buy. Except the answer isn't to poach demand at the last minute. The answer is to redefine the market into something much smaller and more manageable."[6]

That doesn't mean frame-of-mind awareness isn't an approach worthy of your attention—it is. But it's only half the story.

A Sea of Inputs Are Weakening the Grasp of Search

Beyond not being an opportunity to generate demand, searching (in the classic Google and Bing sense) also suffers from a diminishing impact on our purchase decisions. From 2004 to 2011 the percentage of consumers citing "search engine results" as the way they typically found websites declined from 83 percent to 61 percent, according to Forrester Research.[7]

In seven years the role of search engines in locating websites has declined by nearly one quarter. How can that be? Are we less inquisitive? Are we visiting fewer websites? Are we searching less overall? No, no, and no. The reality is that from 2004 to 2011 there has been a massive increase in the

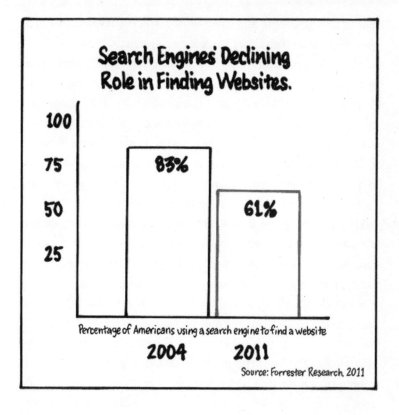

Search Engines' Declining Role in Finding Websites.

Percentage of Americans using a search engine to find a website

Source: Forrester Research, 2011

number of other places we can get website suggestions. The funnel of recommendations—traditionally dominated by Google—is fragmenting like a star going supernova.

If I wanted to buy luggage and preferred to buy or at least research the purchase online (which I did last summer in preparation for a family trip to Greece and Spain), where else could I find a reliable website? Options might include the question-answering site Quora (quora.com). Or YouTube (owned by Google). Or Yahoo! Answers (answers.yahoo.com), an enormous consumer Q&A database. Or ChaCha, a question portal that also enables inquisitions via text message. Or I could just grab my iPhone and ask Siri, the voice-activated assistant built right into the device's operating system.

Why do you think Apple bought Siri? (It's important to remember that Apple bought Siri and incorporated it into Apple's iOS.) Did they buy it because it's a nifty gadget that nobody else had so they could sell more iPhones? No. Siri isn't about selling hardware; it's a Trojan–horse Google killer. When you ask Siri for a recommendation, when you ask Siri for what restaurant to go to, when you ask Siri to find you a website that sells luggage, who are you not asking? Google (or Bing). The more people use Siri on an iPhone, the less people use Google on an iPhone. Google and Microsoft have, of course, been working on very similar technology. Google has years of Google Voice data to use as raw material, and now, not coincidentally, allows for free phone calls from within Gmail. With more voice data to mine and match, voice may be the next great technology battlefield. The number of combatants expanded with Amazon's purchase of text-to-speech firm IVONA in January 2013. IVONA is already used to provide Siri-esque features on Amazon's Kindle platform, and may become a mainstay of a future Amazon smartphone.[8]

In addition to Quora and Siri and the rest, the gorilla that is fulfilling more and more of our recommendation needs is, of course, Facebook. Increasingly, when we want a recommendation for which someone we know may be a credible source, we connect those dots in social media. A 2012 study from Edison Research entitled *The Social Habit* found that among Americans who use social media, more than 30 percent say social media has driven an actual purchase.[9] See this Facebook post from Ann Handley, chief content officer for MarketingProfs, as an example.

I am not suggesting that social is supplanting search, but it is most definitely augmenting it, and the search engine players know it. Microsoft owns part of Facebook and has a very cozy data relationship that incorporates Facebook results (exclusively) into Bing search results. Google's attempts to gain a foothold in social are almost comically earnest, and some would say ham-handed.

As a marketer or business owner, the challenge is to understand that just because your customers and prospects are still using search engines doesn't mean they are only using search engines, as was predominately the case in 2004. "To say that search is the most often used part of the consumer journey should not negate the importance of the rest of the consumer journey," says Tom Webster, vice president at Edison Research. "It may be fact that the consumer journey is 'Hey, I need this, so I asked my friends on Facebook. They recommended a brand, so I Googled it to find their Web address.'" [10]

Webster sees real issues with the misapplication of correlation and causation in determining the impact of search on business. "In our flawed attribution models, Google often gets the credit for the click and the sale, but search is often functioning as a tool or method of convenience, rather than a circumstance where because of the great search engine, and the great search-optimized website, I found a great product."

Well-known search engine marketer and strategist Gord Hotchkiss agrees. "One of the problems with search," he says, "is we have this paradigm where we go to Google, we put a query in and we get a page of results, and we choose a destination. I personally believe search is going to become less of a destination, and more of a tool." [11]

Neither Webster, Hotchkiss, nor I believe that search as a *behavior* will wane, but rather that search as a *place* will. We can search on Quora, Siri, ChaCha, YouTube, Yahoo! Answers, Twitter, Facebook, Pinterest, TripAdvisor, Yelp, Foursquare, and many, many other sites.

The difficulty is that those websites and applications—especially those with heavy social components—have to eventually branch out beyond the classic "you search, we provide results" schema that has remained fundamentally unchanged at the behavioral (if not algorithmic) level for a decade.

Facebook's attempt to marry search and social with its "Graph Search" feature is an early preview of how consumers may use relationships and common interests as key methods of seeking and finding information, goods, and services.

Rob Garner, vice president at global search marketing agency iCrossing and board member of the Search Engine Marketing Professionals Organization (SEMPO), sees this as an evolution from classic search to network analysis and organization.

"All this social data we have, and all this web data, it has to be organized and it has to be sorted. We have to be able to sort through reviews and recommendations and decisions in some way, whether it's a star-rating system, or popularity, or through rankings of personal authority, or membership history, or something else. . . . If you think about it," he continues, "network analysis of this type is like search, but without the query. It's search in reverse."[12]

Frame-of-mind awareness has served marketers well, from the early days of Yellow Pages to the current days of inbound marketing. It will continue to do so, but it's not all-powerful, and it now needs to share the stage with other forces that impact consumer recommendation and preference. Most important among them is a whole new way to market, Friend-of-Mine Awareness.

CHAPTER 3
Friend-of-Mine Awareness

T op-of-mind awareness is an overripe banana, tenuously clinging to relevancy. Frame-of-mind awareness is an apple, worthy of eating, but not enough to sustain you. Luckily, colossal shifts in how, where, and why consumers access information have made a new, third marketing method possible.

I call this friend-of-mine awareness, and it's predicated on the reality that companies are competing against real people for the attention of other real people. To succeed, your prospective customers must consider you a friend. And if, like their friends, you provide them real value, if you practice Youtility rather than simply offer a series of coupons and come-ons, they will reward your company with loyalty and advocacy, the same ways we reward our friends.

Personal and Commercial Relationships Have Merged

Like never before in the history of business, our personal and commercial relationships are merging and entangling, line for line, pixel for pixel. When I looked at my Facebook news feed recently, the first thing I saw was a status update from my friend Chris Moody, a community manager for the software company Redhat Linux, about his son: "In less than a month, my little man will be 1 year old. Crazy how fast it has gone by! Dad Life."

Next, I saw a post from marketing automation software company Marketo, promoting a blog post titled "How to Get More Out of Your Content Promotion." I am drawn to this post because it incongruously uses a photo of Honey Boo Boo as accompanying artwork.

The next item was from my wife, who was being particularly forthcoming about the new schedule she will have when school starts for our kids. "Not doing well with this getting up early thing," she writes. "I think we're in big trouble when school starts in a couple of weeks."

Completing my cross section of four consecutive news feed items was another photo, this time from the New Media Expo conference, linking to a compendium of blog and podcast coverage of their recently completed event.

Let's recap. My Facebook feed looked like this: Friend . . . Company . . . Spouse . . . Company. I'll bet yours looks somewhat similar, as, according to 2012 data from Edison Research, 76 percent of American social media users have "liked" a brand on Facebook.[1]

What you have is an intermingled mixture of information that matters to you because of personal relationships, and information that matters to you because of commercial relationships. It's not just Facebook, either. Twitter works the same way, as do YouTube, Instagram, Pinterest, e-mail, blogs, and podcasts, too. For the first time, companies have to compete on the very same turf as our family and friends, using the very same tools and technologies and media and messaging as consumers.

My wife doesn't buy radio ads to try and get my attention. My friends don't buy newspaper ads. My pal Chris Moody does not buy outdoor advertising or try to optimize his content so that I see it. But the opposite is most definitely true. Companies are now invading the spaces and mechanisms that we're using to connect personally.

Two Ways to Conquer the Invitation Avalanche

Consumers are being subjected to an invitation avalanche, with every company of every size, shape, and description asking people to like them, follow them, friend them, click, share, and +1 them. This is in addition to the interruption marketing tactics and findability campaigns already in existence. At best, it wears thin. At worst, it does more harm than good to brand equity and contributes to the distrust of business spotlighted in Edelman's Trust Barometer.

There are only two ways companies can differentiate themselves within this din and derive meaningful business results. The first is to be disproportionately amazing, interesting, human, wacky, irreverent, or timely. This is where advice to "humanize" using social and new media stems from. It's also the wellspring that feeds the quest to deliver knockout customer experiences—doing so creates "buzzworthy moments" that boost awareness and loyalty. It's where real-time "newsjacking" (as David Meerman Scott calls it in his book by the same name) comes into play—where you listen to the zeitgeist so aggressively, and where your organization is tuned so perfectly, that you can capitalize on opportunities in an instant. It's at the heart of the pitch-perfect and real-time Oreo response to the Super Bowl blackout, whereby the brand created an image of a lone cookie in shadows and the headline "You Can Still Dunk in the Dark." The image captured the moment perfectly, and immediately went viral, with tens of thousands of shares on Facebook, Twitter, and beyond.

All of that makes you smile, and it can create a psychological bond of kinship and recognition that yields loyalty and advocacy among consumers. I believe in the premise of amazing, interesting, human, wacky, irreverent, or timely so much that I cowrote a book in 2010 that is partially devoted to it—especially the human and timely components. But here's the truth: I've worked with more than seven hundred companies as a marketing consultant, and I've come to realize that while "be amazing" can work, it's also extraordinarily difficult.

Telling someone to be amazing is like telling someone to make a viral video. There's no such thing as a "viral video." There are videos that become viral, but they are few and far between. The marketing of "be amazing" is the marketing of the swing-for-the-fences home run hitter. There are two by-products of that approach: an occasional home run, and many strikeouts.

You can do better. You can break through the noise and the clutter and grab the attention of your customers by employing a different approach that is reliable, scalable, functional, and effective.

It's simply this: stop trying to be amazing and start being useful. I don't mean this in a Trojan-horse, "infomercial that pretends to be useful but is actually a sales pitch" way. I mean a genuine, "how can we actually help you?" way.

This is Youtility, and, quite simply, companies that practice it are followed, subscribed to, bookmarked, and kept on the home screen of mobile devices. Companies that don't . . . aren't. Not because they are worse companies, but because they are trying to create customer connections based on product and price, and customers are both tired of it and able to filter through it more than ever.

My family is useful. My friends are useful. Companies can be useful, too. Will yours?

@HiltonSuggests and the Power of Real-Time Youtility

Hilton Worldwide (the parent company of Hilton Hotels and their sister brands like Doubletree Hotels) has a program on Twitter called Hilton Suggests. In 2012, @LTHouston wrote on Twitter, "Good places to eat near the Magnolia Hotel in Downtown Dallas for Saturday?"

@HiltonSuggests answered back, "@LTHouston, Wild Salsa on Main or Campisi's on Elm are awesome, both within walking distance of your hotel in Dallas, enjoy. VAC." (VAC are the initials of the @HiltonSuggests team member who sent the reply.)

Useful and kind, right? But here's the difference-maker: The Magnolia Hotel in Dallas isn't a Hilton property. Hilton Worldwide is going out of their way to provide real-time restaurant recommendations to a person who isn't a current customer.

But someday, @LTHouston is going to be in a different city, and she's going to need a hotel, and she's going to remember the help that @HiltonSuggests provided.

Nearly two weeks earlier, in a different city, Melanie J. aka @RockstarExtreme wrote on Twitter, "Anybody know who's hiring in Orlando for professional positions at this time? It seems like it's at a standstill."

@HiltonSuggests answered back, "@RockstarExtreme, Check out OrlandoJobs.com for a comprehensive list in Orlando."

Now, if I were @HiltonSuggests, I would have said, "Hey, Melanie J., maybe one of your problems is that your Twitter handle is @RockstarExtreme, and perhaps that's not sending the best signal to potential employers." But that's why I'm not in customer service.

Melanie J @RockstarExtreme   8 Jul
Anybody know who's hiring in Orlando for professional positions at this time? Seems like it's at a standstill...
Expand

Hilton Suggests @HiltonSuggests   9 Jul
@rockstarextreme Check out orlandojobs.com for a comprehensive list! #Orlando ^SB

But, if Melanie J. manages to get a job and has money to travel, and she's going to stay in a hotel, where do you think she's going to reserve a room? Hilton.

The @HiltonSuggests program is currently a pilot initiative in approximately twenty-five cities worldwide with high levels of leisure travel. In each, Vanessa Sain-Dieguez, the social media director for Hilton Worldwide, worked with local hotel managers to find employees who wanted to listen and help on Twitter. The tweeters aren't all professional question answerers, either. In fact, few of the @HiltonSuggests team are from the concierge desks of the participating hotels. Perhaps even more unexpectedly, many of them had no prior experience on Twitter. They're just hotel employees who love their city and want to help visitors better enjoy it.

And there's no question Hilton understands and is thinking about the long-term benefits of Youtility, especially unexpectedly. "I think that's actually our biggest opportunity, when we reach out to someone who's staying at a competitor's property or not staying with Hilton," Sain-Dieguez says. "That's where we can make a difference, because they're not experiencing our hospitality within the hotel, and if you're not in the hotel, you may not be getting the same service, and we could win you over." But that takes time, she acknowledges. "We're not looking to win your stay on this trip. We're looking to make a real, authentic connection with you and hopefully gain a customer for life."[2]

One of the most critical elements of this program is the way it combines Youtility and a human touch. Twitter is a personal channel, and Hilton is essentially eavesdropping strategically. That could be misinterpreted if the payoff was more robotic and less deft. Most travel and hospitality organizations would think about a program like this and then try to jump into conversations on Twitter with an exhortation to download an official visitors' guide or mobile application. To not do so was a very specific choice made by Hilton.

"The whole idea there is, you might say, 'I'm looking for a restaurant,' and I could give you twenty options. But they may not fit what you're looking for, and you have to sort through those options," Sain-Dieguez explains. "So we teach the team to ask questions about specifics like, 'Are you with your spouse? Are you looking for kid friendly? Do you want to go somewhere inexpensive?' Then, based on their feedback, we can make a real recommendation."

This isn't just a hospitality program, either. While of course the @HiltonSuggests team provides traveler recommendations most often, they are taught to help wherever they can. Perhaps the best example of this ethos came in the early days of the initiative, when a Memphis resident tweeted that his dog was sick, and he didn't know where to take it for care. The @HiltonSuggests representative in Memphis saw the tweet, knew a vet that he liked, and supplied the vet's name and address. Everything worked out fine, and the dog owner tweeted afterward how amazed he was that Hilton would take the time to recommend a vet to him. That's friend-of-mine awareness with real staying power.

"It's funny," says Sain-Dieguez. "When you help someone and they come back and say thank you, it kind of sets off endorphins or something. The team gets really energized by it, so I think it almost makes them even more eager to look a little more broadly beyond travel, and see where they can help. It's really worked out very well."

She recognizes that the economic impact of @HiltonSuggests is small in comparison to the company's overall marketing efforts. But she believes Youtility pays long-term dividends.

"It's a huge value to the consumer to know, 'No matter where I am, no matter what brand I'm staying at, I can still ask @HiltonSuggests because they helped me in the last five cities I was in.' That's tremendous."

Tremendous, indeed.

Phoenix Children's Hospital Car Seat Helper and the Power of Removing Indecision

Phoenix Children's Hospital creates marketing people want. People would probably even pay for it if asked, but the hospital gives it away. They've tapped into a universal worry among vehicle-owning parents: finding the correct car seat for their child. Parents dread making a misinformed choice about anything related to the safety of their children, and the array of car seat models, sizes, and options is dizzying. Phoenix Children's Hospital helps parents make sound car seat decisions with their free Car Seat Helper app, available for Apple- and Android-powered smartphones and tablets.

The award-winning application is simple, singularly purposeful, and highly effective. Parents enter the height and weight of their child, and it instantly recommends the appropriate type and size of car seat.

"So many people have their car seats installed wrong," says Allison Otu, formerly the media relations specialist for the hospital. "At twenty-two pounds, all of a sudden you're supposed to get a new car seat. Is it front facing, rear facing? Then you walk into Babies"R"Us and it's so overwhelming . . . there are forty-five car seats in front of you. You're not sure what to do. That's one of the reasons this has been so successful, because it's such a real-life application."[3]

Phoenix Children's Hospital didn't have to determine which car seats to recommend, as that information was already published by the American Academy of Pediatrics and being handed out to parents in printed form by the hospital's Injury Prevention Center. Instead, the Car Seat Helper app makes needed information far more accessible. It's an important distinction, because Youtility doesn't always require creating helpfulness from scratch. Taking what already exists and putting it in an inherently more helpful format can be just as effective.

Brian Berg, founder of the mobile marketing consultancy MediaKube and creator of the Car Seat Helper app, says, "The American Academy of Pediatrics recommendations came in a three-page flowchart of medical speak. There's no way anyone could make heads or tails of it. PCH thought it would be a really great opportunity for an application, to make it easy to use."[4] Berg's design converted the flowchart and its logic into the application, making the entirety of the data available via a simple, four-question interface.

In addition to recommending types of seats, the application includes information about car seat recalls and video instructions for safe installation. It's been downloaded tens of thousands of times and carries a 4.5 (out of 5) rating in the iTunes store. If you've used this application, live in the Phoenix area, and something unfortunate happens to your child (she breaks an arm, gets the measles, or something else requiring a hospital visit), are you going to go to the nearest clinic? No, you're going to go to Phoenix Children's Hospital, which is utilizing Youtility to deepen bonds and break through the squall of marketing noise faced by consumers—especially parents.

The impact of the program spreads far beyond the natural geographical boundaries of the hospital, however. "We've had responses from police departments, fire departments, and public safety officers from New Jersey, from California, from all over the place that have found this app, are downloading it, and even using it in their own safety training," Berg says.

It's creating a ripple effect of recognition for Phoenix Children's Hospital, which competes with other major children's hospitals across the country for grants and donors. "It's really extending the reach of the hospital beyond Phoenix," says Berg. "When these other organizations have their own events, they'll use this app as an educational tool, and encourage parents in other parts of the country to download it, because the information isn't Phoenix-specific."

Charmin's Sit or Squat and the Power of Answering a Universal Question

I'm not sure what it is about restrooms that make them so utterly fascinating to some young boys. When I was between the ages of eight and eleven, my family made a summer vacation pilgrimage each year from Arizona to Nebraska. On the way to visit relatives, my younger brother asked to stop at nearly every restroom along the way. You'd have thought each gas station, truck stop, Stuckey's, or map-festooned rest area was a Disney-produced wonder given his constant enthusiasm for them.

History repeats itself. Or maybe it's genetic. My own son has now claimed the scepter and sash as champion family-restroom hunter. Alas, he has many chances to defend his crown. He's a travel hockey player, so on ten weekends each winter we pile into the car and head out for a semi-obscure town in Indiana, Ohio, or Kentucky for games and tournaments. Unlike my mother, who sadly had to endure my brother's fervor for the loo in a pre-Internet age, my wife has a secret weapon: the Sit or Squat app from Charmin.

Sit or Squat is a hilariously useful application for determining the relative suitability of public restrooms. Put in an address or location on your Apple or Android device, and a map appears featuring toilet paper rolls that are either green (sit-worthy) or red (definitely a squat). Grey rolls have insufficient data to make a determination. Users of the application can rate restrooms, and even upload photos to add a layer of verisimilitude to the proceedings.

And when faced with the paradox of choice that is the toilet paper aisle in my local grocer, I don't always choose Charmin, as sometimes I'm seduced by sales and special offers. But I always remember Charmin, and think of the Sit or Squat app every time I see their products. Youtility doesn't overcome all other product and price dynamics, but it gives the brand that extra edge, the tiebreaker that allows it to ultimately sell more by "selling" less.

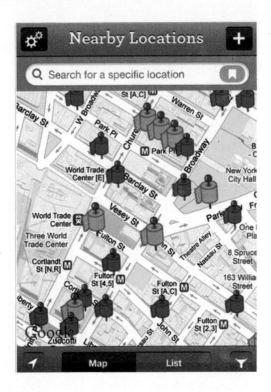

The current version of the Sit or Squat app debuted in 2012 and, like the PCH Car Seat Helper app, has been lauded as worthy in dozens of parent-oriented magazines and blogs. But long before this app, Charmin had a commitment to potty-related Youtility.

"For years, Charmin has been dedicated to meeting consumer needs with clean public restrooms," says Laura Dressman from the Family Care Communications department of Procter & Gamble, manufacturer of Charmin. "This commitment started in 2000 with 'Charminizing' public restrooms at state fairs, then the mobile unit 'Potty Palooza' from 2003 through 2005, and from 2005 through 2010 the Charmin Restrooms in Times Square, which offered clean, free, and family-friendly stalls during the busy holiday shopping season."[5] (Hey, Laura, can we get some of those delivered to ice rinks in Kentucky?)

Because it relies on input from the pottying public to populate its database, Sit or Squat gets better as participation increases. According to Dressman, more than 170,000 restrooms have been added by consumers in just six months since its April 2012 relaunch. Some downloaders of the app object to Charmin's data integrations, however, and several poor ratings for Sit or Squat on iTunes center around the requirement for users to connect their Facebook account before leaving a review. This process automatically posts the review to the user's Facebook page (unless they tweak their publishing settings), which can create some awkward moments, even in a social media world where too much information is de rigueur. Said one reviewer on iTunes: "I used this app and the next thing I know my friend is calling me saying, 'You used the McDonalds bathroom?! Gross!' I was soooo embarrassed!"[6]

Charmin, of course, benefits from the awareness of the brand and the Sit or Squat application that occurs when usage is posted to Facebook (the app also requires age verification, and the terms of service allow P&G to upload data to third parties for analysis). But is that increase in awareness and data access worth the ire it causes among a segment of Sit or Squat's downloaders?

This is the slippery slope of Youtility. At some point in the creation of every marketing program that relies on friend-of-mine awareness, you'll be faced with the option of whether to add Trojan-horse elements (like Charmin's Facebook sync and data collection) that make the Youtility more immediately beneficial to the company. Balancing these benefits with the drawbacks of customer backlash and potentially 'appearing disingenuous are important considerations in the planning and execution phases.

Taxi Mike and the Power of Low-Tech Youtility

Youtility isn't solely available to larger companies. Any company, of any size, can achieve friend-of-mine awareness if they choose to do so. I figured this out while on vacation in Canada with my family in the summer of 2010.

Banff, Alberta, is a ski town. Nestled in the soaring Canadian Rockies, it glistens with bars, restaurants, and tourists galore. There are, of course, many, many taxi drivers in Banff, but there's one taxi driver who absolutely understands the power of Youtility. That's Taxi Mike (who also does web design and computer repair).

Four times per year Taxi Mike puts together the *Taxi Mike Dining Guide: Where to Eat in Banff*. If you're a local or a frequent visitor, you might think to visit the TaxiMike.com website. But for tourists, your encounter with Taxi Mike will likely be via a very simple, 8.5-by-11-inch piece of bright yellow paper, printed on both sides.

Taxi Mike updates his guide every quarter with his latest recommendations for best sports bar, hottest nightclub, best place for cheap drinks, and more than a dozen other categories. Taxi Mike makes a few hundred copies, folds them into thirds like a rack brochure, and delivers them to every res-

taurant, hotel, bar, or tourist establishment in the area. You'll see them on counters all around Banff, and if you don't see one in a particular place, just ask. They have them behind the bar, guaranteed. Proprietors want to hand them out because Mike's information is accurate, and just about every place is listed in Taxi Mike's guide somewhere.

He categorizes. He sorts. He recommends. Taxi Mike is a one-man Yelp, but he's not a social network: He's just a guy. And he puts it all together for nearly free—he inserts just a few ads in each edition. The "Where to Eat Guide" is such a hit that Taxi Mike even has groupies, and signs autographs for passengers on occasion.[7]

At the end of a night in Banff, when you've been to six or eight of these places and you think, "Wow, I really should get a cab home," are you going to walk out on the corner and just raise your hand? No. You're going to reach into your pocket and see the crumpled up, bright-yellow piece of paper that has the map of downtown you've been looking at all night and see "Taxi Mike: 760-1052."

Why Isn't Youtility Universal?

Hilton Worldwide, Phoenix Children's Hospital, Charmin, and Taxi Mike are using friend-of-mine awareness to build relationships with their customers and prospects using information. For each of these disparate companies, Youtility works. So why isn't every company doing it? Why aren't you?

In most organizations, there are two barriers standing in the way of this new type of marketing. One is psychological, and the other is operational.

On the psychological front, the truth is that the tenets of Youtility—making your company inherently useful without expecting an immediate return—is in direct opposition to the principles of marketing and business deeply ingrained in practitioners at all levels. As Brian Halligan from HubSpot puts it, "For a CEO, it's hard. They think, 'Oh, gosh, I know that if I hire a telesales rep, I can have them cold call, and it will work. It's worked my whole career.' But then they know in their head that they don't answer the phone if someone calls. But at least it's the devil they know."[8]

We've been trained to think that marketing activities and outcomes follow a linear progression. We've been told over and over that we sell more with bigger budgets and better targeting, and by perfecting the crafts of interruption and inbound marketing. Youtility is something entirely different. It requires companies to intentionally promote less at the point of consumer interaction, and in so doing build trust capital that will be redeemed down the road. Youtility turns marketing upside down, and many businesspeople simply are not prepared to embrace a situation where the time horizon between input and export is elongated. In fact, executives advocating for this strategy often have to expend considerable internal capital to get budget approval for these initiatives—despite the fact that most Youtility executions do not require substantial resources to produce.

Tim Kopp, chief marketing officer of interactive marketing software company ExactTarget, uses the internal credibility he's earned through years of product-oriented marketing to successfully advocate for new marketing efforts that are rooted in helpfulness.

"I have that battle with internal executives sometimes who say, 'This is crazy. Help me understand. Why are we doing this?'" Kopp explains. "I say, 'I'm telling you this is the right way to do it. If I'm wrong, four pieces into it, we'll stop and do it your way. But this is going to be the right way to do it, and the results will speak for themselves.' But if I hadn't already earned the credibility to do it, it would be much harder, because it does feel unnatural and counter-intuitive."[9]

In most companies, creating marketing that customers want is a colossal shift from the norm. As a result, many current programs of this type represent the first time the business has tried useful marketing (Charmin's decade-long embrace is the exception, not the rule). Because there is no internal history with it, the operational barrier to Youtility centers on roles and responsibilities. Who should be in charge of this? Marketing? Customer Service? Some other department? Further, the execution of Youtility marketing can require expertise in areas that are unfamiliar, such as mobile application development, robust blogging, and tight social media integrations. In chapter 8, we'll discuss how to find the right platform for your useful marketing, and in chapter 10 we'll cover the important role of employees and insourcing.

The Three Facets of Youtility

As you'll continue to find in this book, there are dozens of companies helping customers and prospective customers make better decisions, and benefitting as a result. These examples come from all across the business spectrum, from large to small, global to local, companies that target business customers, and those that target consumers directly, software to retail to services to manufacturing. But there are three distinct facets of useful marketing. Not every program will include all of these; in fact, very few do. But every successful Youtility features at least one of these three approaches, each driven by huge shifts in consumer behavior.

The first is self-serve information: Giving people the opportunity to inform themselves how and when they wish, instead of giving them information funneled through contact mechanisms of the company's choosing.

The second is radical transparency: Providing answers to nearly every question a customer could conceivably ask—before they think to ask it.

The third is real-time relevancy: Using geolocation and other specific circumstances to become massively useful at particular moments in the life of the customer, and then fading into the background until the next opportunity to help arises.

In the next section we'll learn about these three conditions and their important roles, and look at many examples of companies that implement them.

PART II

The Three Facets of Youtility

CHAPTER 4
Self-Serve Information

We've always tried to build loyalty with customers through personal relationships, by being kind, present, and human. From Dale Carnegie's classic *How to Win Friends and Influence People* to the work of sales trainer extraordinaire Zig Ziglar to modern approaches like *Trust Agents* by Chris Brogan and Julien Smith and *The New Relationship Marketing* by Mari Smith, you could fill an entire library with books about the role of personal connection in business. But all of these are now outdated, not because their messages or principles are flawed, but because technology adoption has profoundly altered how consumers interact with information and with businesses. Within the past twelve months we've reached a tipping point that fundamentally changes how companies can market their products, forever shifting the role of reationships and salespeople in just about every business.

We've always tried to build loyalty with people, and we can no longer rely on that technique. Now, we must build loyalty with information.

The Zero Moment of Truth and the Flood of Customer Inputs

In March 2011, Google asked a third-party research firm from Atlanta, Georgia, called Shopper Sciences to conduct field interviews with five thousand shoppers who had recently made a purchase in one of eleven different product categories, ranging from automotive to restaurants. The results were analyzed and turned into the groundbreaking book *Winning the Zero Moment of Truth*. Written by Jim Lecinski, Google's vice president of U.S. Sales and Service, the *ZMOT* book (www.zeromomentoftruth.com) has in short order become a talisman for many digital marketing practitioners, especially those (like me) interested in how the balance of persuasive power is moving from promotion to information.

You know what a moment of truth is. It's when a prospective customer decides either to take the next step in the purchase funnel, or to exit and seek other options. A moment of truth occurs when a clerk asks you if she can help you find something, for example. It's the commercial version of the fight-or-flight response. Let's call it the buy-or-bail decision.

But what is a zero moment of truth? Many behaviors can serve as a zero moment of truth, but what binds them together is that the purchase is being researched and considered before the prospect even enters the classic sales funnel. It's researching a style of jeans before you get to the mall. It's asking your friends on Facebook what kind of contacts to buy, as we saw Ann Handley do in Chapter 2.

Lecinski provides these examples of zero moments of truth in the book's introduction:

- A busy mom in a minivan, looking up decongestants on her mobile phone as she waits to pick up her son at school.
- An office manager at her desk, comparing laser printer prices and ink cartridge costs before heading to the office supply store.
- A student in a café, scanning user ratings and reviews while looking for a cheap hotel in Barcelona.
- A winter sports fan in a ski store, pulling out a mobile phone to look at video reviews of the latest snowboards.
- A young woman in her condo, searching the web for juicy details about a new guy before a blind date.

Zero moment of truth is that instant when you grab your laptop, mobile phone, or some other wired device and start learning about a product or service (or boyfriend) you're thinking about trying or buying.

In its research, Google found that 84 percent of shoppers said ZMOT shapes their decisions,[1] and the new mental model introduced by the research is now standard-issue training for all Google employees worldwide.

There's a lot of fascinating data in the study, but perhaps the most salient to Youtility creation is that in 2010 shoppers (across all categories) needed 5.3 sources of information before making a purchase decision. In 2011, just one year later, shoppers needed 10.4 sources before making a purchase decision.[2]

In twelve months, customers' decision-influencing data needs doubled, and that number will continue to increase in the years to come. Perhaps not forever, as there is both a practical and physical limit to how much information we can parse before buying something. But if your company isn't trying to win the zero moment of truth, you're losing customers you didn't even know you had a chance to get.

What's behind this trend? Why do shoppers need twice as many inputs to make a purchase? It's not that we're less decisive. The truth, as usual, is much simpler. First, we *need* more sources of information because we *have* more sources of information. In your pants—or at least nearby—you have close to the entirety of the world's knowledge in a phone not much larger than a playing card. You can access that knowledge in an instant at almost no unit cost, meaning you're not charged materially more each time you do it. In that scenario, why wouldn't you look something up? Why wouldn't you do a little research first?

The domestic tipping point will happen this year, when smartphone penetration in the United States reaches 57 percent.

In fact, at this point, if you make a bad purchase decision of any kind, from a dicey burrito to a vehicle with unreliable air conditioning, you're just lazy.

The burrito example isn't far-fetched, either. The explosion in zero moments of truth and research isn't solely impacting high-dollar, heavily considered purchases. Consider the correlations between price, risk, and research, as illustrated by this chart from *Winning the Zero Moment of Truth*.

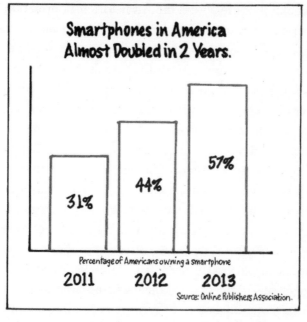

The number of sources needed before making a purchase averages 10.4, but almost doubles to 18.2 if one is buying a car, and decreases to 5.8 before settling on a quick-serve restaurant.[3] That's a big spread, of course, but if the fact that Americans need almost six data inputs before pulling the trigger on a chicken sandwich decision doesn't convince you of the need to win the war of information, I give up.

The second reason behind the rise of the ZMOT is that access to information reduces risk, and that matters to a wide swath of American households. "So your kid has a cough, and you go to Duane Reade or CVS, and what does kids' cough medicine cost? Seven dollars? Eight dollars? Nine dollars?" Lecinski says. "So some of us are probably in the fortunate position to say, 'Well, if I did make a bad purchase, whatever, it's in the back of the medicine cabinet, and I'll go back to CVS and buy a different expectorant, instead of a decongestant.' And life goes on." But, he continues, "The average U.S. household keeps about $39,000 after taxes. Then making the wrong nine-dollar cough medicine purchase is a bad thing."[4]

In his book, Lecinski talks about a combination of forces at play, including the recession and corresponding economic pressures, as well as the realization that products of every type can now be researched and reviewed. To make the point about the pervasiveness of online information, even for inexpensive, everyday products, Lecinski is fond of telling audiences, "There are more reviews for Bounce Dryer Sheets online than there are for this hotel."[5]

It's worth taking the time to research low-cost, disposable goods because the friction and hassle of doing so has dropped almost to zero. Yesterday's librarian is Siri today.

Always-on Internet Access Has Made Us All
Passive-Aggressive

One of the most interesting dynamics of this huge shift in consumer behavior is that while we need more information, far fewer transactions involve face-to-face interactions with other people. This truly is the era of self-serve information.

How many times have you purposefully chosen to not fill out a contact form on a website because you didn't want to be called, or even e-mailed? I'll bet more than a few times. Even if it's a product in which you have a genuine interest, you'll avoid filling out that form until the last possible moment, preferring instead to kick the informational tires yourself. "Smartphone" is a misnomer. We're not using them to make phone calls. A decade ago I easily received twenty or more calls per day. Now, it's three or four. Instead, I have a menagerie of inboxes, with asynchronous messages streamed to me from e-mail, Facebook, Twitter, LinkedIn, Pinterest, Instagram, my blog, and text messages, as well as notifications from topic-specific websites like TripAdvisor.com. No wonder we prefer our information to be self-serve. We want to be left alone!

Usage data proves this point. From 2009 to 2011 American females' use of voice minutes on mobile phones decreased by 12 percent. During the same period their text messages sent and received increased by 35 percent. For men, it increased 44 percent.

And, if middle-aged men like me are going the passive-aggressive, self-serve route, imagine the behavior pattern of tomorrow's dominant consumer cohorts. As chronicled on the blog of Brian Solis, new media pundit and author of *What's*

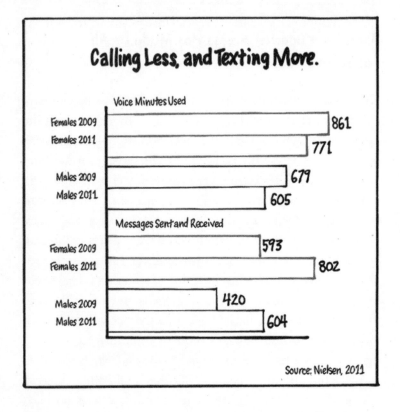

Calling Less, and Texting More.

Voice Minutes Used

Females 2009	861
Females 2011	771
Males 2009	679
Males 2011	605

Messages Sent and Received

Females 2009	593
Females 2011	802
Males 2009	420
Males 2011	604

Source: Nielsen, 2011

the Future of Business?, outsourcing company Sitel and communications company TNS released research in 2012 that determined that 71 percent of U.K. residents between the ages of sixteen and twenty-four will search for a solution online before contacting a company directly.[6]

Generational marketing consultant Kelly McDonald, author of *How to Market to People Not Like You*, believes the impact of mobile Internet is, if anything, being underreported because of the propensity to use average figures to explain the trend. Averages include the mobile Internet usage of people who may never fully embrace it, such as her mother.

"My mom is seventy-six," McDonald says. "It's not that she's a technophobe, but she's never going to be as comfort- able with technology as someone who has not had to adapt to it, who has had it all their lives. Before the Internet, the greatest invention was electricity, but I grew up with it, so I don't appreciate it. I flip the lights on, and they come on. But there was a time when electricity was amazing and awe-inspiring, and it made everything more efficient. So in the same way that our generation takes electricity for granted, younger people today take the Internet for granted, and because they grew up with it, they have no reason to not trust the information they find there. But my mom does not trust it. She doesn't know if her mobile banking deposit 'went through.' She'd rather go to the branch and see them in person."[7]

Death of the Salesmen

We used to talk to a real person as a first step. To get familiar with the company. To learn more. To create bonds. Not now. Now we talk to a real person as a last resort when we've exhausted the supply of ZMOTs and have a query so specific only a human being can answer it.

This is most egregiously true in a category where the transactional stakes are often the highest: business-to-business marketing. In 2011 the Corporate Executive Board surveyed 1,900 B2B customers to uncover insights about purchasing behavior and found that customers will contact a sales rep only after independently completing 60 percent of the purchasing decision process.[8] Sixty percent of the decision is made before the prospect identifies himself. Sixty percent of the decision is made before a call, or an e-mail, or an entry into your lead tracking database. Customers are ninjas now. They are stealthily evaluating you right under your nose.

This has manifest consequences on the role of salespeople, whose job used to be to develop and nurture relationships. No longer. The role of salesperson is now to answer specific questions capably and quickly, and to close deals that became possible due to the self-serve research performed by the customer. What does that 60 percent figure mean for marketers? A lot, according to the Corporate Executive Board's Ana Lapter. "The 60 percent mark is in that part of the mid-funnel that is critical in terms of driving the buyers' consideration of a supplier for a potential purchase," Lapter says. "Therefore, marketing needs to de-emphasize tasks like thought leadership and white papers, and focus more on advanced activities, such as diagnosing purchasing needs and identifying internal barriers to purchase."[9]

Marketing needs less top-of-mind awareness and more Youtility. Sounds about right to me. Brian Halligan at HubSpot agrees, and has seen this shift firsthand:

"I started my career as a sales guy in the nineties. And back then, the whole funnel really was controlled by the sales rep. You're cold-calling somebody, and you kind of manage the process all the way to the funnel. There's asymmetric information. The sales rep has all the information the prospect wanted, including pricing and discount options. You had so much control. Now 90 percent of it has swung to marketing. It's self-service, and you need to be able to be very, very helpful to see to the top of your funnel. The game changed a lot."[10]

Smart companies understand that providing self-serve information and giving consumers the opportunity to find answers for themselves, without being burdened by personal, synchronous communication, isn't shirking their duty as marketers; it's *become* their duty as marketers.

It may seem absurd to suggest that consumers will bypass human contact to make complex, expensive purchases. But it shouldn't. Founded in 1999, Blue Nile is the largest online retailer of diamonds in the world. Who would buy a diamond ring, necklace, or earrings online without ever seeing them in person? Evidently, lots of us . . . including me, who bought an anniversary diamond ring for my wife. In 2012, Blue Nile posted more than $400 million of annual revenue.[11]

Also consider the case of eBay Motors, the Internet's largest marketplace for automobiles and accessories. As of the second quarter of 2012, 4.62 million vehicles have been sold on eBay,[12] with more than 75 percent of those sales conducted interstate. How busy is the eBay Motors marketplace? A motorcycle is sold every seven minutes and a Ford Mustang is sold every forty-nine minutes.

Beyond changing the role of salespeople forever, this shift alters the way companies organize their products, provide customer assistance, and recommend vendors.

Life Technologies Offers
Self-Serve Information Through Interactive Video

Global biosciences company Life Technologies operates in a business category not typically known for its cutting-edge use of YouTube, nor its embrace of new marketing principles. But in 2011, Life Technologies launched the most quintessentially useful video program with the best utilization of video annotations I've ever seen. (Annotations are words or

phrases embedded in videos that serve as a call-to-action, and sometimes provide a direct link to other videos.)

Their "Interactive Selection Guide to Immunoprecipitation" (ar.gy/lifetech) is actually forty-two short videos chained together with an elaborate annotation scheme, giving Life's customers—working scientists—an easy, self-serve way to determine which products are the best fit for the job.

According to Oslo-based Andrew Green, Life's divisional lead for Video and Interactive Marketing, the original plan was to create a customary, web-based product finder. Realizing, however, that online arrays of pull-down menus and such are ultimately devoid of personality (and only passively educational), they decided to build it entirely in video, where they could better anticipate some of the questions customers might have, and actively incorporate them.[13]

Mapping the content and determining how the videos would connect and branch was the most difficult part of the project, says Green—who sent me a photo of the wall-sized chart they used to plot it all out.

The videos have accumulated more than seventy-five thousand YouTube views, which is truly extraordinary, given their extremely narrow customer target.

Clorox Gives Away Self-Serve Stain Information

In 2009, David Kellis, the director of PR and Social Media for Clorox, along with his colleague Amanda Mahan, began to research how consumers were searching for stain solutions online. Two important findings become immediately apparent. First, there were thousands of searches being performed about stains. And second, Clorox wasn't coming up in the search results, despite having a laundry product that's been a household staple in the U.S. for a hundred years.

"When we saw that," Kellis says, "we thought there was an opportunity for us to provide specific advice on how to remove certain kinds of stains on certain kinds of fabrics. But with the popularity of smartphones and the iPhone, we thought we'd be able to provide people with stain advice on the go, when stains actually happen, whether you're eating in a restaurant or in a park, or just places where you're not necessarily near your laundry machine."[14]

Thus was born the Clorox myStain application, available on smartphones and tablets. It includes a very large directory of common stains and remedies, and a link to the web-based "Dr. Laundry" for more detailed information.

The combination of the two resources, one an on-the-go mobile directory, the other a more personal, in-depth blog format, provides Clorox customers with a self-serve option

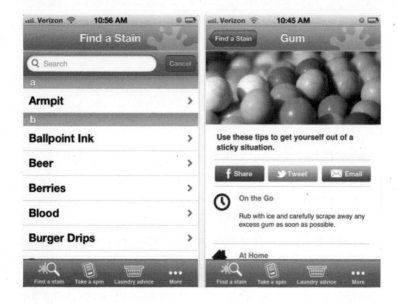

that fits whatever their current situation might entail. Dr. Laundry was the precursor of the myStain app, and actually predates it by nearly three years. "Dr. Laundry" is not a made-up character, either. She's a real person (and a real doctor), a former scientist for Clorox who was consistently being asked by her neighbors how to attack a panoply of stains, and who decided to make stain advice a career.

One of the differentiators between the app and Dr. Laundry is that on her blog Dr. Laundry often researches her own advice and reports back to readers via follow-up blog posts. "She takes every question very, very seriously," says Kellis.

The stains covered in the myStain app are purposefully more likely to occur in public, helping users navigate the sometimes confusing, and seemingly contradictory, conventional wisdom about what to blot and dab with what. In many of those out-of-home circumstances, and even in some

in-home stain situations, products from Clorox may not always be the perfect remedy. Impressively, the app is quite
candid about this. It's not a sales pitch for Clorox; it's an
interactive directory of highly useful information.

"We knew that on-the-go people don't carry Clorox
around with them. But even at home, there are some stains
that our products don't work that well on," says Kellis. "But
we wanted to provide a solution anyway, because we wanted
to be authentic and not turn this into something that just
sold our products, but was actually a valuable tool that was
also entertaining. So, as stain solutions came up, we'd run it
through our claims department, or legal, or even Dr. Laundry
and say, 'Hey, how are we with butter?' and she'd say, 'We're
terrible with butter.' But we didn't want to not have butter
in our app."

Kellis acknowledges that other corners of the company
didn't universally see the wisdom in adding stain removal
tips that did not include Clorox products. Eventually, however, the goodwill associated with being a more comprehensive, less brand-centric, application became the preferred
direction.

As of fall 2012, myStain has been downloaded more than
175,000 times and won the 2012 Appy Award[15] from industry
journal MediaPost as the best branded content application.

Big Poppa Is a Conduit for Self-Serve Information

In some cases you don't have to provide all of the information prospective customers will access in their zero moment
of truth—you just need to provide the mechanism for that
access. Sometimes just facilitating self-serve tendencies is

as good as fulfilling them. Sterling Ball is the master at this approach.

A man of many talents and interests, Sterling is the president and CEO of Ernie Ball, one of the largest and most historically important manufacturers of guitar strings and related equipment. Founded by Sterling's father, the eponymous Ernie Ball, the holding company also makes electric and bass guitars and runs a series of highly successful music festivals, including the country's largest Battle of the Bands.

But it's Sterling's hobby that got him to practice Youtility. He's always had a passion for outdoor cooking, and living in southern California provides him ample meteorological opportunities to pursue it. Using his e-commerce, marketing, and distribution experiences honed in the music business, he founded BigPoppaSmokers.com, a website selling barbeque smokers and accessories. Beyond selling the high-ticket hardware, Sterling (whose nickname is, of course, "Big Poppa") sells sauces, spice rubs, gadgets, and even fine meats . . . all of it online.

In both verb and noun form, "barbeque" properly refers to meat cooked at low temperatures for a long time over wood. What most people do in the backyard is "grilling," which is cooking fast and hot over charcoal or propane. I know this because I am a barbeque hobbyist—a card-carrying member of the Kansas City Barbeque Society and a certified barbecue judge. That's how I found Sterling. I purchased a ridiculously elaborate (but truly awesome) pellet smoker from BigPoppaSmokers.com in 2012. Pellet smokers are a type of smoker that use small wooden pellets made from compressed sawdust as their fuel source, rather than the sticks and logs used in classic smokers. It makes the cooking more reliable and idiot-proof, perfect for an attention-deficient novice like myself.

Sterling is more than a merchant, however. A few years ago, Sterling decided to move his own cooking from the backyard to the big time and started a competition barbeque team called Big Poppa Smokers[16] (naturally). He and employees from Ernie Ball formed a traveling team that journeyed across the western United States, competing for thousands of dollars in weekend showdowns against dozens of other teams to see who could create the tastiest ribs, pork, chicken, and beef brisket. Sterling's oversized personality and comfort with the media and marketing even landed him a recurring role on TLC's reality television show about the circuit, *BBQ Pitmasters*. He's currently sitting on top of the barbeque world after winning the American Royal Invitational contest in October 2012,[17] the World Series of meat smoking.

Thus, as it turns out, I learned to cook barbeque from the very best. I didn't learn this directly, though Sterling is very generous with his recipes and knowledge. I learned because I spent an inordinate and indefensible amount of time reading PelletSmoking.com, Sterling's companion site to BigPoppaSmokers.com. PelletSmoking.com is nicely designed and easy to use, but under the surface, it's a self-serve throwback. It's not a blog or a Facebook page or a YouTube channel. It's just an online discussion forum where people like me who own newfangled pellet smokers congregate to swap tips, photos, advice, and tall tales. Presently, there are 5,236 discussion threads, 59,182 posts, and 2,371 registered members of the site. And just about all of them buy their gear from Big Poppa.

Before I bought my smoker (the Memphis Elite from Hearthland Manufacturing), I did extensive research on makes and models, which is how I found the PelletSmoking.com forum. I spent several days there, reading dozens and dozens of questions and answers. And when I knew what I wanted, a purchase at BigPoppaSmokers.com was literally a click away, and I continue to purchase there almost exclusively.

An important note about Sterling's model of facilitating self-serve information is that communities don't thrive on their own. Big Poppa and his small team of employees participate in the forums constantly. Each day they are answering questions, cajoling, encouraging and fostering a sense of communal spirit that keeps people coming back to learn—and to buy. There is tremendous market research potential in this level of engagement, and as Sterling has written on his blog, "I want to get as close to my customer as possible, so I can smell their breath. . . . Why? Because I still share their passion. Because I get direct feedback on what the diehards are thinking."

Angie's List: Youtility from Day One

Sterling Ball takes a somewhat organic approach to self-serve information and uses it to drive commerce and loyalty. Conversely, every molecule of Angie's List, a fast-growing reviews and recommendations membership community, is devoted to information and Youtility.

Venture capitalist Bill Oesterle refurbished an old Victorian home in Indianapolis, and to help do so successfully joined a loose collective called Unified Neighbors. Unified Neighbors was a club that produced a monthly, printed newsletter and dispensed advice to members about trustworthy contractors and tradespeople. In 1994, after the refurbishing was completed, Angie Hicks, a student at nearby DePauw University, began an internship with Oesterle. Hicks didn't know quite what she wanted to do after graduation, and was pondering a career in finance, so she interned for Oesterle to get some experience in the field.

The next year, 1995, Oesterle moved with his company to Columbus, Ohio. When he began to search for reliable contractors there, he discovered that Unified Neighbors was an anomaly. According to Cheryl Reed, Angie's List director of communications, Bill thought, "Oh, there's one in Indianapolis, there must be one everywhere. There's not? Aha. There *should* be one everywhere."

Oesterle convinced Angie Hicks to run the fledgling company instead of moving to Washington, DC, to start a career in consulting. The rest is history, or history in the making.

"From the very beginning, the service was based on the idea that homeowners needed help in finding good service providers. It's a universal problem," says Reed. "And this is a great solution because the information comes from others who have used the service. It's reliable."[18]

Now with approximately one thousand employees and fiscal year 2011 revenue of $90 million, Angie's List started as something much, much, much smaller—not dissimilar from Taxi Mike in Banff. Angie went door to door to sign up members, and began as a phone-in service. If members needed a recommendation for a contractor, they literally picked up the phone and called Angie. Imagine "Dear Abby"—but for plumber advice and a monthly fee. According to Reed, the name was changed from "Columbus Neighbors" to "Angie's List" because people kept calling and asking, "Hey Angie, can you give me that list?"

The company moved back to Indianapolis in 1999, bought out United Neighbors, and took the concept online. Now, Angie's List operates on a national scale, providing ratings and reviews on more than 550 service categories to nearly two million paying members. Membership grew by 82 percent between fiscal years 2010 and 2011, and the membership retention rate exceeded 75 percent.

The site is exceptionally user-friendly and reliable, with no anonymity allowed, and extensive interaction between contractors and members. "Very early on, we started to encourage service companies to respond to reviews," Reed says, "in large part because that gave the consumer even more information. It gave them both sides of a story. . . . Companies cannot control their grade except by providing good service. So consumers set those grades. Once companies are able to earn good reviews, then if they can keep their grades up, they're allowed and encouraged (they're eligible, but not required) to advertise with us."

Because Angie's List provides such a wide array of information about each service company, members can sift and sort data and make decisions based on criteria that suit their particular circumstances. Members can sort by grade: "only show me electricians in my area with average grade of 'A.'" They can also sort by proximity to the member's home, by discounts offered, by company name, or by recency of reports.

Beyond the website, Angie's List is available via smartphone and tablet applications, and still maintains a physical call center. "Back in the day, it was Angie answering the phone. It's still human beings in the call center six days a week because sometimes, let's say your basement's flooded and you need help right away, you probably don't want to sit down at your desk in the basement and do your research to find a good company," says Reed. "You can just call us up and we'll do it for you."

The explosion of Youtility to help us make better decisions, from Google to Angie's List, has fractured the consumer pur-

chase funnel, and there will be no repair. If you don't supply the information your prospects need to choose your company over the competition, they'll get that data somewhere else, and the outcome might not be as favorable for you. To win the zero moment of truth, you need to fight the war of information on home turf. One way to do that is through the provision (or facilitation) of self-serve information. But there's another way that's perhaps less self-serve, but equally useful—answering every single question your prospects might conceivably have.

CHAPTER 5
Radical Transparency

I know a lot about Arizona. I lived there from 1970 until 2010, with residences in Lake Havasu City, where I was raised, and where the "falling down" London Bridge of nursery rhyme fame was rebuilt in 1973 as a tourist attraction; Tucson, where I went to university; Phoenix and various suburbs; and the mountains of Flagstaff, where one year my family and I received 120 inches of snowfall at our house.

After experiencing just about all the Grand Canyon State has to offer, my wife and I decided in 2010 to consider other locations. I'm a marketing consultant, author, and speaker (which may be replacing actress/singer/model as the most common triple threat job description in America). Consequently, I'm fortunate enough to be able to do my work more or less anywhere. This realization, and the inkling to possibly

act on it, was the zero moment of truth for my eventual re-
location.

I didn't participate in Google's research, but if I had, I'm
certain I would have pushed up the average on number of
sources needed to make a decision. I research vacations ob-
sessively, read many product reviews on Amazon and elsewhere, and consume blog posts like Halloween candy. I draw
the line at chicken sandwich investigation, however, preferring the visceral thrill of fast food drive-through roulette. In
short, there's usually a method to my madness. So when we
considered moving from Arizona, the obvious next step to
me was to research our options. We created and ranked a list
of desirable attributes: college town, fewer than two hundred
thousand people, close to a major airport, in the middle of
the country, good schools, decent weather, affordable cost
of living, and other factors. Then, we turned to the Internet.

We used a variety of websites that compare, contrast,
and recommend locations to narrow down our list. Most
notable among them is BestPlaces.net, the online home of
researcher Bert Sperling's "Places, USA" software. This system, first developed in 1985, allows people to enter their personal preferences to find their own best place to live, work,
or retire. Almost every time my wife and I performed these
analyses, Bloomington, Indiana, was recommended by the
location-finding websites. I'd never been to Bloomington,
and I had only a vague understanding of where and what it
was through my consulting work with ExactTarget (located
one hour north in Indianapolis) and the film *Breaking Away*,
which chronicles Indiana University's Little 500 bike race
tradition. This lack of knowledge was not a deterrent. "I'm
an online marketer," I thought. "Who am I to argue with a
carefully researched relational database?"

So, off to Bloomington we went, knowing nothing and nobody. We fell in love with the city on our visit, and, three months later, we sold our home in Arizona, hugged friends and family good-bye, and drove across the country with two kids, a dog, a cat, a snake, a lizard, and twelve cases of wine to start our Indiana experience.

Without BestPlaces.net there is no chance I'd be writing this chapter in the law library of Indiana University in Bloomington. None. In fact, friends who cannot fathom that I'd pack up and move based on a website joke that BestPlaces.net must be a guerrilla marketing program created by the Bloomington Chamber of Commerce. Not true, but a great idea!

If BestPlaces hadn't answered most of my questions about how Bloomington compares to other cities, I never would have gotten past the zero moment of truth. For me and my family, BestPlaces was the ultimate Youtility. Creating customers by answering their questions is imminently viable and carries remarkable, persuasive power. If you need evidence of the potential impact of the approach, re-read the foreword from Marcus Sheridan, whose commitment to answering every customer question not only saved his business, but catapulted River Pools into a market-leading position.

Holiday World and Splashin' Safari— Answering Questions You Didn't Know You Had

Not far from my new home in Bloomington lies Santa Claus, Indiana, home to Holiday World, one of America's best, and best marketed, amusement parks.

Founded by Evansville, Indiana, industrialist Louis Koch as a retirement project in 1946, Holiday World is the world's oldest family-owned theme park and has been continuously operated by the Kochs for more than sixty years.

The original catalyst for the park's construction was a misleading place name. Koch was troubled that the village of Santa Claus was a disappointment to children who found the environs to be utterly devoid of St. Nicholas. First named "Santa Claus Land," the attraction included a toy shop, toy displays, themed children's rides, and, of course, Santa himself. In 1984 amenities were expanded to include Halloween and Fourth of July themes, and the name was changed to Holiday World. The Splashin' Safari water park was added in 1993. In 2006, the combined Holiday World and Splashin' Safari won the coveted International Applause Award, which is given each year to an amusement park "whose management, operations, and creative accomplishments have inspired the industry with their foresight, originality, and sound business development." Holiday World is the smallest park ever to receive the honor, and was also named the "World's Friendliest" and "World's Cleanest" amusement park in 2010.

As a three-time visitor, I can attest to the family-friendly and highly efficient atmosphere at the park, which features three buzzworthy attributes that are very unusual in this age of nickel-and-dime tourism. Holiday World and Splashin' Safari offer guests free parking, free soft drinks, and free sunscreen. The cost of these items is microscopic compared to the goodwill they produce, and you've never seen a happier ten-year-old than one with unfettered access to water slides and soft drinks.

As sound as the operational side of Holiday World is, their information and question answering is even more noteworthy. The park's website, HolidayWorld.com, may

not win any design awards, but it is probably the most useful online resource for any attraction, anywhere. Holiday
World embraces the premise that no question is unworthy
of an answer, and that filling information gaps is of equal
importance to promotion and chest-thumping. Dozens of
pages on the site are devoted to when to go, where to park
and what to expect. Most people go to amusement parks
infrequently, especially combination land/water parks, so
there are a lot of visitation details to be considered, and
Holiday World proactively provides answers to questions
that many visitors wouldn't even think to ask—until they'd
walked through the gates.

Their commitment to transparency extends to each ride as
well. For every major attraction at Holiday World and Splashin' Safari the company provides an array of detailed data about
the ride, including a historical narrative from Holiday World
scion and former president Dan Koch, and as many as five videos showing the entire experience from different perspectives.
Featuring several of the world's longest wooden roller coast-
ers, these videos do an outstanding job of either persuading
fence-sitters that they can handle the ride, or convincing them
they most definitely cannot. Here's a super slow-motion, high-
definition version: ar.gy/holidayworld.

The ride descriptions on the website are a trivia geek's
dream. Here are the massively specific ride facts provided
about "The Voyage":

TYPE: Wooden out-and-back coaster, steel structure
OPENED: May 8, 2006
VEHICLES: Two PTC trains, holding 24 passengers each
THEME: Named for the heroic voyage of the Pilgrims to
America in 1620

DESIGNER: The Gravity Group plus Will Koch
TRACK LENGTH: 6,422 feet (1.2 miles)
HEIGHT: 173 feet, highest to lowest point on the ride
RIDE TIME: 2 minutes, 45 seconds
TOP SPEED: 67.4 mph
WORLD RECORD: The Voyage provides the most air-time of any wooden coaster: 24.3 seconds (anything less than +.25 vertical G's, average front/middle/back seats).
BANKING: Three 90-degree banked turns
TUNNELS: Record five underground tunnels, including eight "underground moments" and a "triple down" feature in one of the return-run tunnels.
LIFT HILL: The lift hill measures 163 feet.

Pilgrims? PTC trains? Speed measured in tenths of a mile per hour? +.25 vertical Gs? Most amusement parks would try to get by with "must be forty-eight inches to ride, but it's really, really fun."

Holiday World and Splashin' Safari innately understand that you need to let customers in on the behind-the-scenes details. Today's consumer wants to see the metaphorical sausage being made. Or even the actual sausage, as Holiday World is one of the very few amusement parks to post all of their restaurant menus and prices online. It's a guest service, says director of communications Paula Werne. "We're not ashamed of our prices. We're not trying to hide anything. The people who want to plan their day can plan their day. 'Well, we're going to have pizza at Kringle's Kafe for lunch and then at supper we're going to go to Plymouth Rock Cafe and have turkey dinner.' They love budgeting it out ahead of time."[1]

It's not just "content," it's a commitment. "The primary focus is to create the best possible guest experience on the day of visitation by giving them directives about rides, ride heights, ride restrictions, show times, foods that are available, allergen-friendly menus, and tips for a better visit," Dan Koch tells me. "We want to give them as many tools as we can within the website, without being overly complicated, so that the guest has a real good working knowledge of how to have the best possible day at Holiday World when they choose their day of visit."

The most important aspect of Koch's description of their information mission is his emphasis on creating the best possible experience. The focus of the website isn't selling the attraction, getting visitors to come back a second day, or selling T-shirts. It's about using information to improve customer experience, which creates loyalty and word of mouth. And it's working. Of the 643 reviews of Holiday World and Splashin' Safari on TripAdvisor, 608 are four or five stars.[2] Recognize that unless it inhibits ease of use, there is no downside to providing this level of radical transparency to your prospective customers. Werne says she's never been told, "You're giving us too much information." Each day they even post the water temperature at Splashin' Safari to the website and to Twitter where, of course, they were the first amusement park to have an account.

Your Customers' Expectations Are Changing

As this point in the book you may be thinking "Youtility is interesting, but nobody in our industry is doing that kind of thing, so why should we start?" Here's the secret: Your industry isn't relevant. What matters instead is that other companies are embracing Youtility, and, in so doing, they are changing the expectations of your customers, whether you like it or not. It doesn't matter whether anyone in your industry is doing real-time question answering like Hilton Suggests. Hilton and others are, and thus they are training consumers to think of Twitter like a telephone. It doesn't matter whether anyone in your industry is providing self-serve information like the myStain app. Clorox and others are, and they are training consumers to expect this type of lightly branded information that helps them solve problems and answer questions without buying a thing.

It has always been this way. I remember in 1998 when I was a web strategist and Amazon rolled out a new navigation scheme on their website that featured tabs to switch between sections.[3] This kicked off an entire era of tabbed navigation for websites of every size and category. It didn't matter whether a competitor in *your* industry had tabbed navigation; it mattered that a site as prominent as Amazon did.

"There are some verticals that have tended to be pioneers in providing online functionality, online information, and transparency," says search marketing strategist Gord Hotchkiss. "What happens is consumer expectations are being set by those front running experiences, and now they're expecting those across all verticals, and a lot of companies are struggling with that."[4]

Going even further back, in 1994 I was working at my first Internet company, Internet Direct. On October 27 of that year, Wired (then hotwired.com) launched the very first banner ads.[5] Those banners were 468 pixels long and 60 pixels high because that was the size the hotwired website designer shoehorned onto the home page. And guess what? That became the standard size for the entire World Wide Web, codified by the Internet Advertising Bureau in 1996.

It's an interconnected world. Your customers are impacted by a lot more than just the marketing tactics of your narrow, competitive set. That's why it drives me crazy when I hear complaints like, "These B2C examples aren't relevant to us because we're B2B."

"This whole democratization of information almost becomes an arms race between the company and the consumer," Hotchkiss says. "As expectations on the consumer side rise more and more, companies embrace that and start becoming more forthcoming with information, and providing functionality online . . . which again raises consumer expectations."

You can't be afraid to be the first one in your industry to embrace these principles. That's why I'm so enamored with the McDonald's Canada question answering program. It doesn't matter that you're probably not working for a fast food company; the Golden Arches' embrace of information could be the start of a cultural change that impacts every business and makes Youtility a must.

McDonald's Canada Has Nothing to Hide

If Holiday World isn't ashamed of their prices, McDonald's Canada certainly isn't ashamed of their food. Launched in June 2012, their "Our Food, Your Questions" program invites any Canadian to ask any question whatsoever about McDonald's food on their special website. To ask a question participants must connect with either Twitter or Facebook, providing greater visibility and a ripple-in-the-pond viral effect, as questions appear on the inquisitors' social network. Within the first seven months 19,000 questions were asked, at a rate of as many as 450 per day. In that period more than 12,000 questions were answered.

The program is only dedicated to McDonald's food, so questions about nonfood topics are directed to other resources, and some questions are of course duplicates. But there's no dodging the tough questions, and that's the most amazing element of this program. McDonald's Canada is addressing head-on the rumors about food quality and safety that have dogged the brand seemingly forever, accentuated in this real-time, veracity-challenged world where mistaken reports of celebrity deaths on Twitter are a seemingly daily occurrence.

As an example of the types of questions McDonald's is going out of its way to address, take this zinger from Jani S. in Nova Scotia: "When you say 100 percent beef, do you mean the whole cow: the organs, snout, brain, kidneys, etc. or just the plain beef we buy at the grocer?"

Whoa. Historically, companies would do whatever possible to put as much distance as possible between themselves and that line of inquiry. But the rules are changing. Here's McDonald's answer—comprehensive, factual, and not laden with artificial marketing hype: "Hi Jani. We wouldn't call it plain beef, but it sure is beef. We only use meat cut from the shoulder, chuck, brisket, rib eye, loin, and round. In fact, our beef supplier is Cargill, a name you might recognize. They're the biggest supplier of beef in Canada."

Or this one, from Isabel M. in Toronto, who asks, "Why does your food look different in the advertising than what's in the store?"

In that response, McDonald's writes: "Hi Isabel. Thanks for your question. You're right, it does look a little different. But rather than us telling you with text, let our Director of Marketing, Hope Bagozzi show you why in this video." The embedded, three-and-a-half-minute video thanks Isabel for the question, and shows the details of an actual photo shoot, demonstrating the dark arts of food stylists and retouchers. The video makes it clear that all the ingredients used in the commercial are exactly the same as those used in the restaurants, but it acknowledges, with almost shocking candor, that the product is heavily manipulated for the cameras. A hit on YouTube, the video has generated nearly 7.5 million views (ar.gy/mcdonalds).

What effect do those millions of views have on perception of McDonald's as a brand? According to Joel Yashinsky, chief marketing officer for McDonald's Canada, the impact will be long-term trust. "We knew you're not going to get an immediate return on investment. But we believe that the return on investment will be over the long-term, because it's going to grow our brand trust and brand health. What I like to call the 'love of the brand' is going to get much stronger, and in the end, we all firmly believe that the return is going to be greater than the investment . . . it's going to be such an important part of our culture moving forward."[6]

Already the brand is seeing reputation gains. In pre- and post-consumer research conducted after the first phase of the program (before significant advertising dollars were expended to drive awareness), the "curious skeptic" segment of McDonald's prospective customer base gave the company 16 percent higher marks for "good quality ingredients," according to Yashinsky. Other areas where consumer agreement spiked included attributes like "being genuine" and "improving nutritional content" and "food I feel good about eating."

For many companies, a question answering program like this might fall into the category of reputation management, and might task company representatives with answering questions from consumers wherever they occur: Twitter, Facebook, blogs, forums, and the like. In McDonald's case, this is not feasible, as the volume of chatter about the brand is too pervasive and widespread. "We have to use the channels we own so that we can have a conversation with customers, because there are so many different channels out there that we just can't physically reach all of them," Yashinsky says.

And while building a centralized destination for question asking and answering may have been operationally required for McDonald's, it's an approach that has strategic advantages for all companies.

"If you can build the platform where you become the trusted expert, you can literally sell anything," says Joe Pulizzi, founder of the Content Marketing Institute and author of *Get Content, Get Customers*. "If companies had more people thinking about that instead of focusing on the product all day long, I think it would open up all kinds of opportunities."[7]

One major opportunity this centralized approach offers is an audience for Youtility. Could McDonald's Canada have created a big effort around e-mailed questions or built a new food-oriented call center, like the Butterball Turkey Talk Line?[8] Sure, but those options don't have the benefit of answering questions publicly. Information provision is now a spectator sport, and McDonald's not only understands this important trend, but has also built technology to capitalize on it. I especially like that they provided an option for website visitors to "follow" a question and be notified when it has been answered. While it's no doubt impressive that more than nineteen thousand questions have been asked so far, it's far more impressive (and beneficial to McDonald's) that 6.5 million questions have been read.

I asked Yashinsky why every company isn't doing something like "Our Food, Your Questions." "I think everybody's going to start," he said. "We knew that there was really no option if we were going to become a brand of the twenty-first century, as we were of the twentieth century. The customer today wants to know more, especially about the food that they're eating."

McDonald's is effectively balancing the need to promote with the need to inform, a symbiosis that Yashinsky says is very much intentional. "If you have a good story to tell, tell it. But you have to do it in a way that's authentic, and you have to have that conversation with the customer. You can't just preach to the customer these things that you know are true. You have to engage them, so that they can come to learn and believe it and build that trust with you."

Warby Parker Answers Questions Every Which Way They're Posed

McDonald's Canada has created a specific platform and protocol for answering customer questions, providing the company a meaningful dose of control over sequencing, which questions are answered, and other operational details. Given the scale of the effort and the number of questions asked, having a defined mechanism for answers is probably a requirement. But smaller companies are increasingly answering every consumer question regardless of where and how it is asked.

"Our philosophy is that we would never ignore a phone call or an e-mail, or somebody that walks through the door of our showrooms, so why would we do the same with a tweet?"[9] says Jen Rubio, head of social media at Warby Parker, a manufacturer and retailer of eyewear whose commitment to transparency and Youtility is disrupting the industry.[10]

Fashionable Warby Parker frames cost just $95 with prescription lenses, and the company donates a pair of glasses to a person in need every time a pair is sold. How can the company afford to offer such low prices? First, the markup on eyeglasses is significant, and the company is willing to operate on lower margins. Second, Warby Parker's customer-acquisition costs are kept low by selling mostly online, and using Youtility to drive exceptionally high conversion and loyalty ratios.

Not unlike buying a swimming pool online from River Pools and Spas, or buying an engagement ring online from Blue Nile, purchasing eyewear over the web is novel for many, and question-filled for all. "There's so many things you can do to make buying glasses online easier and faster," says Rubio. "A lot of it we do now. Nobody ever has their

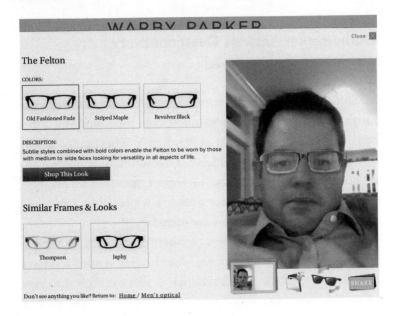

prescription, so we'll call your doctor for you and do that. Buying glasses is one of the most intensive, highest-touch retail experiences out there."

Warby Parker is trying to replicate that experience by removing the friction and psychological barriers that inhibit Youtility. In addition to a detailed FAQ similar to Holiday World's, the company has a virtual showroom on the website where potential customers can use the camera on their computer to "try on" frames. Once choices are narrowed down using the virtual try-on, the company offers a free, home try-on program where prospective customers can order up to five frames (without prescription lenses) to be sent to their home for a trial run. Once the home try-on is received, many customers (including me) create videos of themselves in each pair, and upload the options to the Warby Parker Facebook page, where employees and fans comment on which look best. For less decisive potential customers, Warby Parker answers selective tweets with custom YouTube videos (ar.gy/warby), where they discuss the comparative merits of different frames.

"If the answer is something difficult to express in 140 characters on Twitter, we love taking it to video," says Rubio. "We've had people go, 'Oh. Your model on the website is a brunette, but I'm a blonde. How do those glasses look on a blonde?' We'll then have someone in the company model them in a video."

Freezer Burns: Answered Questions, Created an Industry

"You are in two businesses," Joe Pulizzi says. "You're in the 'whatever business you're in' business, and you're in the media business."[11]

Greg Ng lives, breathes, sleeps, and eats this dichotomy. But mostly, he eats. Ng is the founder and sole proprietor of *Freezer Burns*, a video blog devoted exclusively to reviewing frozen foods found in supermarkets in the United States.

In 2008 Ng had recently moved to North Carolina to start a new job as an online marketer[12] and was waiting in line with five coworkers to use the single microwave in the company kitchen. He said to himself, "Why do you think this person chooses this? Why did this person choose this other one? It would be interesting if there was a review site for frozen food."[13]

Ng was inspired by Gary Vaynerchuk, whose video blog about wine, *WineLibraryTV*, helped increase revenue at his family-owned wine shop tenfold, catapulted him to a ten-book publishing contract, and helped secure a national radio show on SiriusXM. Vaynerchuk delivered a stirring, much circulated keynote speech at the Web 2.0 Summit in October 2008 that became a touchpoint for an entire collective of new information entrepreneurs like Ng. Subsequently outlined in his book, *Crush It!*, Vaynerchuk inspired Ng and others to follow their passion and take advantage of their evening hours to add structure to their enthusiasm.

"Gary talked about getting rid of excuses, and that seven p.m. to two a.m. is plenty of time to do damage," Ng says. "The same night I saw his speech, I shot my first episode, and I haven't looked back since."

That's a bit of an understatement, as *Freezer Burns* celebrated episode 575 in November 2012, and recent iterations of the very short (three to four minute) show are generating as many as 250,000 views each, across thirty different video networks.

Ng sells advertisements on his video and blog, and major consumer packaged goods companies pay him to honestly re-

Amy's Mexican Casserole Bowl Video Review (Ep554)

Posted by: Gregory Ng: The Frozen Food Master

Recommend | 2 | Send | SUBSCRIBE ON YouTube

view their new offerings. "I don't do paid endorsements . . . and I try to be as objective as possible," Ng says. "At the same time, there are companies who have new products, or new product lines, or new brands that want to get some exposure. So I charge for a guaranteed review within thirty days, with the disclaimer that I may like it, or I may not like it."

This forthrightness is one of Ng's success secrets, as his core audience of college students and lower-income Americans don't want to waste money on a poor choice within a category with a bewildering array of ever-changing options. He's not afraid to pan an item that deserves it, and his compilation of "The 5 Worst Tasting Frozen Foods" is featured on the home page of the blog, which also includes the complete archive of every review he's done.

Similar to the success of McDonald's Canada, the depth of content Ng has accumulated on the blog contributes to its momentum, like a self-fulfilling prophecy of information and frozen lasagna. According to Ng, about 60 percent of the visitors to the blog are new each day (meaning they haven't been there in at least 30 days), and approximately 10 percent of his visitors on a given day will consume 18 pages or more on the blog. This is the same dynamic that Marcus Sheridan explained in the foreword, with River Pools and Spas customers reading blog post after blog post after blog post until they've sufficiently scratched their zero moment of truth itch.

These aren't isolated success stories either. More questions answered equals more success in an equation that is almost wholly linear. Interactive marketing software company HubSpot analyzed data from more than seven thousand companies and found that companies (both B2B and B2C) with 101 to 200 pages on their website generated two and a half times more leads than companies with 50 pages or fewer.

Every page on Ng's site is found by Google, visited by prospects, and shared in social media, creating an information annuity that generates ongoing benefits. In most cases, these increased page counts are derived through the type of aggressive blogging that Ng and Sheridan prescribe. To pay real dividends, blogging and question answering has to be a significant, robust effort. More and more companies are embracing blogging as a way to communicate with customers and prospects. Seventy-seven percent of B2B companies surveyed by Content Marketing Institute and MarketingProfs in 2012 were using blogging as a marketing tactic. But how many of those blogs are crafted with the obsessive commitment to question answering you'll find on *Freezer Burns* and River Pools? Being comprehensive makes a difference. The more questions you answer, the more useful you become, which breeds visibility and loyalty. In the same study, HubSpot found that companies that blog fifteen or more times per month get five times more traffic than companies that don't.

Success won't come overnight, but it will come. Ng says his first fifty episodes of *Freezer Burns* averaged 200 to 300 views within the first week of airing. Now, however, new shows generate one hundred thousand or more right away, and even his first shows have slowly accumulated many, many views over time.

Answering Questions with Advocates

Fully committing to answering customer questions can be a lot of work. But one of the ways you can reduce the operational impact on your business is to imbue your existing fans and advocates with permission—implicitly or explicitly—to answer questions on behalf of the brand.

This happens organically for many companies, and always has. But more recently, thanks to the development of social media–listening software, we have the ability to more easily find these moments of questions being answered by fans. In fact, a study by ExactTarget of the "Hot 100" retailers with e-commerce sites found that 51 percent saw fans answer customer questions on Facebook before the brand itself could answer.[14] In some cases, your fans are not only willing to answer questions on behalf of the company, but are doing so more nimbly.

Beyond an open forum like Facebook, brands can facilitate this scenario by creating—and more importantly, nurturing—invite-only communities of customers where the back and forth is a bouillabaisse of best practices, how to's, product ideas, and support requests. ExactTarget maintains such a community. Called 3Sixty, it's the online clubhouse for current customers, enabling them to interact with one another as well as with a large cross section of employees. Product enhancements are recommended and voted on by 3Sixty members, impacting the company's development road map. As Jeff Rohrs from ExactTarget explains, where you answer questions online in many ways dictates the overarching purpose and usefulness of that initiative, and the outcome varies from channel to channel.

"The ExactTarget Facebook page is our most emotionally connected place online. It's largely lightweight, but there's some viral stuff there. Whereas our 3Sixty user community is very much around peer-to-peer and brand-to-peer, customer service, self-service, and education," says Rohrs. "It's the community space where we can truly help people improve the performance of their programs."[15]

Beyond the organic, volunteer nature of customers answering questions among themselves (a dynamic that's very strong on many discussion forums, like PelletSmoking.com), some companies are formalizing this role, putting advocates to work in a more official capacity. This is essentially a postmodern version of America Online chat room moderation. Fifteen or more years ago, when AOL was booming and had thousands of active chat rooms, the company could not afford to pay people, even at minimum wage, to manage each chat room, some of which were devoted to exceedingly arcane topics. Instead, AOL recruited consistently active, seemingly sane and stable participants in each chat room, elevating them to the role of moderator, which was, of course, an unpaid promotion in most cases. History repeats. Today there are companies that will recruit current customers and super fans and train them to answer the questions of prospective customers via e-mail and live, online chat. Who better to educate and persuade potential buyers than someone who has been through a similar scenario?

It was two years before Gregory Ng even thought about monetizing. Many of the other companies profiled so far are very much looking at their new friend-of-mine awareness initiatives as long-term plays. Are you and your company willing to wait that long? It requires a fundamental change in business mindset to embrace Youtility, but Geek Squad, Hilton, McDonald's, *Freezer Burns*, and more are proving it can work if you have patience.

Sometimes, however, you can create Youtility in a faster, more visceral way. To do so, you have to understand not just how to be useful, but where and when.

CHAPTER 6
Real-Time Relevancy

Youtility today may not be Youtility tomorrow. In a particular scenario, your marketing may be so useful that your customers and prospects want it and might even pay for it if asked, yet in a different environment that same marketing has negligible value. If you're walking around downtown Banff, Alberta, the Taxi Mike map and dining guide is gold. When you get to the next town, it's recycling. With marketing of this type, your success is scenario-specific, which is why it's so critical to be truly, inherently useful. If you are, your audience will keep your marketing close—on their home screen, in their inbox, in their Twitter and Facebook feeds—and, when they need you, they'll access whatever it is you're bringing to the information party. You don't have to be "found"—at least not after initial discovery—because your customers and prospects already know where you are and what you offer. When they need you, they'll engage.

There is no courtship, ramp up, or slow build with Youtility. You're either sufficiently useful at any given moment, and thus can connect with the customer, or you're not. It's real-time relationship building. Once you have new glasses, your ability to get questions about them answered by Warby Parker becomes a less fulfilling proposition. Until, one day, you need new glasses again, and then you'll know where to turn. Meanwhile, they have your money from the first purchase and are patiently waiting for your needs to realign with their usefulness.

Like an endless game of informational hide-and-seek, Youtility consists of popping out from behind a tree to assist when necessary, then fading back into the woods to wait for the next opportunity.

This staccato and circumstantial relationship between company and customer is the by-product of a movement that has fragmented brands and made the notion of "greater than the sum of its parts" an anachronism. The branding ligaments that for decades created cohesive corporate attributes have been surgically removed. Brands have rushed to provide value (optimally) or promotions (typically) on every new communication platform, all of which are increasingly accessed through mobile devices, making customers' relationships with brands solely a collection of micro-experiences. This is the "app-ification" of brand value.

What do I think of Hilton as a brand overall? I don't have many feelings about them at that level, and I'm a Hilton Honors member. But my relationship with the company isn't at the brand level, it's at the granular level. To me, Hilton is judged by Hilton Suggests, their Facebook interactions, their Pinterest board, their Instagram efforts, and by how useful their e-mails are to me. I'm almost certain that I've never viewed a single page of the Hilton website, other than the room-reservations engine. But I've digested almost the entirety of their mobile and social media programs and will continue to do so . . . when the time is right.

For decades, the key question has been "how valuable is the brand?" The key question moving forward is "how valuable are your apps?" Apple, of course, started this trend with the introduction of the first iPhone, but distilling entire companies down to a collection of utilities is now pervasive, and that is where the vast majority of technology and marketing development is headed. When fully implemented, this atomization of brand value will make the web far less valuable than it is today, and will make real-time relevancy via Youtility the primary battleground for all companies.

George Colony, chief executive officer of Forrester Research, has been sounding this alarm for years. He calls the trend the "App Internet" and believes it will usher in a new breed of corporate winners and losers in every category:

"As the Web becomes the AM radio of digital, the mobile App Internet will rise. This market will be dominated by two or three ecosystems—semi-closed worlds built on a closely fitting set of apps, phones, tablets, computers, operating systems, and partners," writes Colony on his blog. "It doesn't matter what you sell—insurance, pills, cars, energy, bonds—you'll be reaching many of your customers through these ecosystems in the future."[1]

The rampant proliferation of mobile, high-speed Internet access is responsible for this evolution, and the magnitude of the mobility behavior shift cannot be overstated. According to projections from Morgan Stanley Research, by 2014 there will be more mobile Internet users than desktop Internet users.

According to Apple, the company sold more iPads in April through June 2012 than any computer manufacturer sold of their entire product line.[2] The shift away from the web and toward mobile apps will be massive and fundamental. Already, app usage is a daily reality for many mobile users, and research firm Gartner, Inc. estimates that total app downloads will increase more than 600 percent between 2012 and 2016, reaching an astonishing 309 billion per year worldwide.[3]

The international nature of app-ification is important, as the United States is by no means a leader in mobile devices or mobile high-speed Internet access. As of November 2011, the International Telecommunications Union estimates there were nearly 2.9 billion mobile cellular subscriptions in Asia and the Pacific, compared to 969 million in the Americas.[4] But more important than the number of users is the more critical role mobility plays in information and commerce in areas of the world beyond the United States.

"The online Web is less advanced in Asia than in North America or Europe," wrote Rohit Dadwal, managing director of the Asia Pacific section of the Mobile Marketing Association in a 2011 interview.[5] "This means that mobile is *the* mode of communication across key Asian markets. Millions more Indian consumers can be reached through mobile than through TV, for example . . . Meanwhile, in the developing countries, there's a whole class of people who don't have access to bank accounts, and the needs of this unbanked sector are being met through mobile—it is a great example why mobile innovation and advances in Asia really matter—it's just not the same in North America or Europe because the same needs do not exist."

Aaron Strout, head of location-based marketing for digital marketing agency WCG, agrees that the United States has

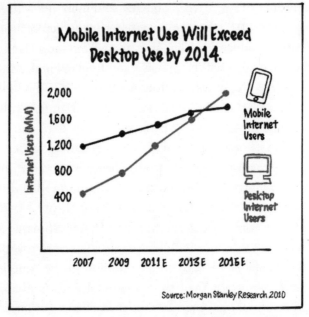

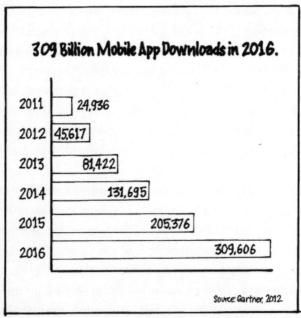

catching up to do in mobile. "We absolutely are laggards, and desktops and laptops slowed us down. Terrestrial wifi and Internet access slowed us down. Whereas places like Korea and Japan leaped right to the phone, and places like Brazil leaped right to the phone, and they are a couple of technology generations ahead of us," says Strout. "Will we ever catch up?"[6]

Not only is the mobile research and commerce lifestyle more ubiquitous in other areas of the world, it is also more ubiquitous among today's younger consumers. The Social Habit research found that more than 41 percent of twenty-four- to thirty-five-year-old American social media users with a smartphone purchase products directly from that device at least monthly,[7] compared to 16 percent of forty-five- to fifty-four-year-olds who also use social media and don't own a smartphone. Today's younger consumers aren't just researching and buying via mobile either. The app-ification of brands is actually more persuasive to this generation than other forms of marketing. In an amazing 2012 study, SymphonyIRI found that Americans in the Millennial generation are almost four times more likely than American consumers overall to have their purchases influenced by smartphone applications.[8] The impact of these apps on their purchase decisions is greater than recommendations from blogs and social media, and from manufacturers' websites or e-mail.

Within a generation every customer and prospective customer of every company in every developed nation will have never known a world without the ability to access information at any time through a mobile device. A popular 2011 YouTube video uploaded by UserExperiencesWorks called "A Magazine Is an iPad That Does Not Work" (ar.gy/ipad) provides a fascinating and visceral examination of this reality. In the clip, a one-year-old child is shown navigating an iPad with seeming purpose and facility, and, when given a magazine, immediately attempts to access its contents via touch and pinching movements.

There are three ways to provide real-time, circumstantial Youtility. The first is to be useful based on the customer's location. The second is to be useful based on the customer's situation. The last is to be useful based on seasonality or external factors.

In nearly every case, app-ification and providing value via mobile is the easiest path. When using a mobile device, customers and prospective customers are often sending a steady stream of information about what they might need. Tapping into a consumer's location and then providing geography-specific usefulness is the most common way companies can be helpful in a mobile context. Many of our most used applications—like Google Maps—rely on it. Each time Google Maps prompts you to get driving directions from "your current location," Google is polling your mobile device and using geolocation to create usefulness. We may not always perceive it, but this is a massive advance over the previous generation of way-finding that required you to know your current position to plan a route.

Meijer Saves Shoppers Time with In-Store Mapping

Sometimes you need to plan a route not across town, but across a store. That's where the Meijer Find-It application becomes relevant.

Point Inside is a mobile mapping technology company based in Bellevue, Washington. Unlike Google Maps (and

the new, recently maligned Apple Maps), Point Inside specializes in indoor cartography, providing shoppers with en-
hanced experiences. In 2010 the company partnered with
Meijer, a family-owned, Michigan-based retailer with more
than two hundred stores in the Midwest, to develop the
industry's first mobile product locator. The typical Meijer
store includes more than one hundred thousand items: a mix
of grocery, hard goods, and soft goods. Jeff Handler, former
chief marketing officer for Meijer, became aware of Point
Inside's indoor mapping technology and wondered whether
it could be applied in a retail environment. The resulting
collaboration became the Meijer Find-It app, a mobile locator for Apple and Android devices that provides real convenience to shoppers.

Within Find-It (ar.gy/meijer), consumers can locate specific products anywhere in the store (to within a few feet), view
and clip virtual coupons, create and track personal shopping
lists, route a trip within the store to maximize efficiency, locate store services such as restrooms, and view items currently on sale. There is also a built-in locator showing all Meijer
stores across the country. A short demonstration video on
YouTube (ar.gy/finditdemo) shows Find-It at work, and il-
lustrates how easy it is to locate products at the individual
SKU level.

Todd Sherman, current chief marketing officer at Point
Inside, says that providing consumers with the routed shopping trip inside the store defies long-standing tradition, but
it is much in demand among shoppers. "The conventional
wisdom for years has been to put the products people want
in the back of the store. They'll have to walk through the
entire store and something will catch their eye, and they'll
put it in their shopping cart. What's been found is that really

doesn't work. People are kind of in a hurry, and in fact, they get annoyed that they have to walk all the way to the back of the store to pick up the milk."[9]

Sherman and Point Inside claim that many shoppers think about trips in time chunks, and "beating" their presumed time by making that trip more efficient creates additional, spontaneous purchases. "What happens is people go to the store and they have a mental number: 'I've got twenty items. I'm giving myself thirty minutes to shop for them,'" Sherman says. "If you can help somebody pick up those items in twenty minutes, they'll use that extra ten minutes to look at other items in the store and add some of them to their shopping cart."

In a highly competitive retail setting, it doesn't take many instances of adding or subtracting shopping list items to make a material impact on sales and profits. As Sherman notes, if the consumer has twenty items on his or her shopping list and cannot locate one item on their trip, it's a potential 5 percent decrease in revenue, using an average cost across all items. "By bringing the shopping lists into an application that drops pins and shows customers within a couple of feet where each of those products are, it eliminates that 5 percent reduction," he says.

Point Inside continues to build on the original technology deployed for Meijer with new mobile couponing opportunities and maps for major airports and shopping malls. A major new retailer (still a secret at this time) is readying a store mapping application with Point Inside, and, as part of the development process, conducted interviews with shoppers using the pilot version. The potential impact on loyalty is significant. According to Sherman, "Sixty-five percent, I think, of the customers said that they would shop at that store, and not their competitor, because the application gave them the ability to find products so easily."

The Fight Against Show-Rooming

While applications like Find-It provide retail Youtility that can increase average order size and customer satisfaction, a more insidious combination of mobility and location is creating substantial teeth gnashing among some merchants. Increasingly, consumers are using their mobile devices to comparison shop in real time, determining whether the product in front of them on the shelf is being sold for the best price, or whether consumer reviews are positive or negative for the product. Widely known as "show-rooming" in the retail world, it's a phenomenon that's very real. Research from the Social Habit found that 56 percent of American men who use social media and have a smartphone use that device to comparison shop or check reviews when shopping locally. Forty-three percent of women do the same.

Consumers are assisted in this effort by apps that enable in-store browsers to scan the bar code for nearly any product and have prices and reviews from dozens of websites pushed to their mobile device in seconds. Amazon's Price Check application is often used to show-room, and it even includes the option to take a mobile picture of any product, which Amazon will attempt to find, using advanced photo recognition technology. Other options focus on a particular category, including Wine Spectator's mobile reviews application, that provides, for a small monthly fee, the company's full database of wine reviews.

Retailers have been in the habit of "matching any price" for many years, but until recently those offers did not extend to online. Now, show-rooming is forcing retailers like Best Buy and Target to match prices of major online competitors.[10]

Other, more nefarious attempts are being made by retailers to defeat the show-rooming trend, including using store-specific bar codes, disabling Internet access in-store, and using sensors to determine if a consumer is accessing a site like Amazon, and, if so, offering a real-time offer.

But as Steve Deckert, marketing manager for e-commerce loyalty-rewards company Sweet Tooth, writes on his blog, these efforts to defeat show-rooming are "attempting to solve the wrong problem." The problem, he explains, "is not that less expensive products exist, or that customers are able to easily check for less expensive products. The much more dangerous problem is that customers have commoditized your product and brand. Your customers have reduced your brand to a product and a price; you are offering no more value than a vending machine. Retailers and show-rooming solutions that try to prevent consumers from accessing the Internet on their mobile devices are essentially trying to 'battle' the Internet. They will lose. . . . You need to provide value to the consumer other than simply giving them a product at a cheap price. You need to differentiate yourselves to offer value that is beyond a product and a price."[11]

Beauty retailer Sephora, with more than three hundred stores in the United States and Canada, is taking Deckert at his word. Sephora is, somewhat ironically, attempting to differentiate the in-store experience with technology. An iPad application, available only within physical Sephora retail locations, gives shoppers additional product review details, personal shopping histories, and other Youtility features that cannot be replicated with a bar code scanner.[12]

Others, like luxury goods manufacturer Burberry, are attempting to differentiate by making the in-store shopping experience itself powerful and noteworthy in a way mobile devices cannot. As documented on the blog of Pointsmith, a point-of-purchase marketing management company from Texas, the Burberry flagship store is equal parts retail and rock concert.[13] "Burberry's flagship store in London has drawn a great deal of attention, and for good reason," Pointsmith writes. "They have developed an upscale shopping experience that is not only impressive, but also personal for the shopper. Interactive signage greets shoppers as they walk into the store and displays key points of interest within the building. Once in the store, associates armed with iPads containing customer information, such as past purchases and preferences, greet shoppers. Certain clothing and accessories contain RFID chips that allow shoppers to interact with digital mirrors that show videos on craftsmanship or pairing recommendations. The store features digital signage throughout the showroom that shows Burberry fashion shows. Occasionally, there are 'disruptive digital takeovers' where thunder booms out of 500 in-store speakers and all 100 signs and mirrors display an iconic London downpour."

That level of personalization may seem remarkable for an in-store environment, but just wait until it's all around us. That's the future, according to Asif Khan, founder and president of the Location Based Marketing Association. As proof of their concept, Khan's group has been working with transit authorities in New York and Chicago to customize marketing messages every time a bus comes to a stop. "We've taken buses with digital screens on the side, and instead of selling the ad inventory in the normal way based on the route the bus travels, what we do is when the bus stops at a red light in an intersection, we gather all the check-in data of everybody who is standing at that intersection," Khan says. "In real time, we build an aggregate demographics profile, and then we serve an ad on the side of the bus based on who's actually there. And then we do it again at the next intersection when the bus stops again."[14]

Khan says location is a functional layer that will make all kinds of not-yet-envisioned Youtility possible for smart marketers. "It becomes about, 'Well, you know where I am right now, you know where I've been before, and you can know where my friends are and where they've been.' You can infer a bunch of things and kind of get to this point where you can kind of predict, it's almost like predictive marketing in terms of where I am going next," he says. "And if you can do that, location becomes really, really valuable."

Location is a valuable opportunity for marketers, to be certain, but its power must be tempered by providing information and offers that are useful to consumers, not just brands. The tendency to overplay the location hand has resulted in a string of interesting but vaguely off-putting plat-

© marketoonist.com

forms that allow companies to intrude on consumers in new and novel ways. But at least in the United States none have yet reached mainstream usage and acceptance at the customer level.

Vanderbilt CoachSmart App Helps Coaches Keep Players Safe

Location-based usefulness may very well become the most common form of mobile usefulness, but it's not the only alternative. Companies and other organizations are also providing customers and prospective customers with information that's important in particular situations and scenarios.

One of my favorite (and most inherently useful) examples of this form of marketing is the Vanderbilt CoachSmart application. A collaboration out of Nashville, Tennessee, between the Vanderbilt University Medical Center and the Monroe Carell Jr. Children's Hospital at Vanderbilt, the app is becoming a must-have for sports coaches. Available for Apple and Android devices, it provides an array of useful tools to keep players safe. Perhaps the most interesting is a lightning sensor. If lightning strikes nearby, the app sends an alert to the phone and tells coaches what to do next, recommending whether an outdoor practice should be immediately aborted. The app also helps coaches prevent heat exhaustion by providing real-time data on heat, humidity, and the heat index. A comprehensive collection of information for coaches is also included, such as hydration tips, injury prevention guidelines, and concussion symptoms. Coaches can even use the app as a contacts tool, notifying all players (or parents) from within CoachSmart. It's currently in use

by hundreds of sports leagues across the country, as well as two National Football League teams.

The hospitals see the CoachSmart app as building relationships through information that is incredibly important in a defined scenario, according to Jill Austin, chief marketing officer for Vanderbilt University Medical Center. "If you think about where we are in the changing market for health care, we don't know where it's going to end up, but it's obviously changing in terms of health-care reform and how patient relationships get formed and maintained," Austin says. "I think loyalty is going to be the key for those relationships that get formed up in the front end of whatever the new market looks like."[15]

The CoachSmart app was born from a legacy program where athletic trainers affiliated with Vanderbilt went to high school football practices in the Nashville area to let coaches know whether it was safe to practice based on the current heat index. However, according to Betsy Brandes, the director of Web and Creative Services for Vanderbilt, this is an intensely manual endeavor, with trainers having to use specialized monitoring equipment to evaluate safety on the field, since heat indexes can vary significantly within one mile.

"We recognized that there was a need for that type of information for people who don't have access to our athletic trainers," says Brandes, a leader of the team that met with area coaches to determine how a mobile application could make safety information widespread and portable. "Not only was heat index important, but lightning was really important because it's so ambiguous how you determine distance and procedures."[16]

While CoachSmart was developed to serve the needs of coaches in Nashville, it's now being used by a much broader audience. The information it delivers is relevant almost regardless of geography—the opposite of the Meijer Find-It app in that regard.

"The lightning network that we belong to serves the contiguous forty-eight states, so the app works in all of them," Brandes says. "And it's not just for coaches. It can be for canoeists or fishermen or any outdoor enthusiast who wants to keep track of lightning."

While Vanderbilt's patients come mostly from the local region, the spread of the CoachSmart app across the country very much fits into the hospital's larger branding strategy, which, in this instance, was helped by app-ification, not harmed by it. Austin believes that staying on the cutting edge of technology–enabled information provision helps reinforce that Vanderbilt is a leader in medical technology as well.

"It's completely congruent," she says. "Looking at how we put our name out in front of a variety of people across the United States is one of the things we're doing in our national strategy. Apps, by their very nature, are not limited to your backyard, so we count this as part of our national engagement strategy."

The app has been so successful that Vanderbilt is working with the university tech transfer office to make the program revenue neutral by charging a nominal fee for the (heretofore free) app. Usage is so high the fees for accessing the lightning database are becoming costly.

The future of hyper-relevance may be taking applications like this to their logical extreme, using "anticipatory computing" to push information to participants before they even realize they need it.

MindMeld is an iPad application that adds a new layer of Youtility to video conferencing. Using Facebook as a contacts directory, MindMeld users can launch a call quickly. Once the call commences, the MindMeld software listens and pushes useful information like web pages, YouTube videos, and *Wikipedia* entries that will fill in knowledge gaps for people on the call.[17] MindMeld is the first component of a platform being built by technology entrepreneur Tim Tuttle to "continuously pay attention to what happens in your life and pick up ambient information and then start to surface relevant information." Sounds like the greatest research assistant ever.

Dan Deacon Turns Fans into Part of the Show

Youtility isn't all business.

"For the first time, having your phone out at a concert is not a jerk move," says the description of the official app of Dan Deacon, a Baltimore-based electronic musician known for his engaging live performances. Launched in September 2012 to coincide with Deacon's new album and tour, the app is available for Apple and Android devices and turns concert-goers' phones into a synchronized light show, and even into an extra instrument that Deacon can "play" from the stage. A short YouTube video demonstrates the app in action (ar.gy/deacon).

The app has created significant industry chatter for Deacon and the app's creator, Keith Lea, with articles in *Rolling Stone*, *Billboard*, *SPIN*, *CMJ*, and more. Writing in *Forbes*,[18] music blogger Leor Galil called the app a natural extension of Deacon's career-long desire to turn his audiences into a community. According to Galil, Deacon offers his fans a unique concert experience in which the audience is encouraged to participate.

"Controlling a large crowd while trying to engage with it is obviously a difficult obstacle to overcome, which makes the concept of the app so appealing," Galil writes. "Deacon and company have made an intriguing app that begs attendees interested in having an enjoyable concert experience to toss all distractions and notions of how to act at a show aside in order to use it: It invites anyone with a smartphone to participate in a way that asks very little of the most reserved concert-goers in order to get people to collectively come together in a really powerful way."

The technology and story behind the genesis of this example of real-time relevancy is remarkable. Says cocreator Lea, "Me and Dan and Alan Reznick, who is also involved with the app, we were all on a bus together. I was running tech and they were both performing on this little tour around the East Coast. . . . I guess Dan had seen the Beijing Olympics Opening Ceremonies and he saw that they handed out LED bracelets and had them sync up. Dan's idea was why did they bother going through the effort of handing out all of these little LEDs when everybody has, essentially, a little light in their pocket?"[19]

Lea recalls that, as Deacon's "nerdiest friends," he and Reznick were asked about the feasibility of using smartphones in this way, which instigated weekly meetings to work on the project. It turned out to be more difficult than initially imagined.

"You'd think getting a bunch of pretty sophisticated little minicomputers to do something all at once would be easy," Lea says. "We first thought the obvious thing was to use wifi . . . but we called a couple of networking contractors and just none of them had any ideas because of the need to get five hundred to a thousand people on a wireless network that needs to be torn down and put up every night."

After abandoning wifi as the syncing technology, the team considered using existing 3G and 4G cellular networks as a connection point, but realized that access wasn't universally strong at all show locations, and music festivals often feature overloaded cellular networks.

Digging deeper, they took an inventory of all the sensor arrays present across all smartphones and realized, "Oh, well, every phone obviously has a microphone and a speaker," remembers Lea, who used the neolithic days of dial-up Internet connections as inspiration. "Back in the nineties we all got on the Internet through a phone connection, and it's just audio that's being used to transmit data."

With the app installed and running on a smartphone, Deacon can control the devices en mass by playing audio tones that "instruct" the phones to flash, change color, make sounds, and more. It's quite a spectacle, and a surprise even to fans who have downloaded the app and ostensibly have an idea of what to expect. "It's a really cool moment when Dan first plays the tone and then all of the phones change color," Lea says. "Usually people are a little shocked. They're not really ready for it to work. They don't know what it's going to be like. People are used to their phones being magic, but this registers as a different sort of magic."

Deacon and team have no plans to charge for the application, and, while licensing the technology to other artists is certainly a possibility, this is one instance where Youtility isn't about marketing or brand building. "Maybe this is a little trite, but it is pretty cool that a couple of artists and a programmer got together, and with a really tiny budget came up with something that is transforming the way people look at their cell phones in this performance context," Lea says.

Scotts Miracle-Gro Solves Seasonal, Agrarian Problems

The Scotts Miracle-Gro Company is the world's largest marketer of branded consumer lawn and garden products, including the Scotts brand of grass seed and lawn fertilizers, and the Ortho brand of lawn and garden pest-control solutions. The company also has a robust services division that provides regular lawn care to commercial and residential addresses throughout the United States.

With the exception of the Miracle-Gro line of household plant fertilizer and nutrients, the majority of the company's products are used seasonally or circumstantially. Making sure customers understand which product to use in which situation, and when, is a major objective for the company, and they've embraced it in nearly every operating division.

The Scotts brand offers "Lawn Care Update," a monthly e-mail newsletter that dispenses specific, useful, and seasonal lawn and garden advice to subscribers. Operating since 2009, the update is produced in six different regional variations to ensure that the advice is relevant. After all, what Michigan residents should be doing to their lawns in October is far different than what Floridians should be doing at the same time. Beyond the regional editions, the update has even more customization capabilities, as subscribers can specify what type of grass their lawn includes, and other criteria that result in a highly personalized, instructive e-mail delivered to them each month. While the e-mail does recommend which Scotts products to consider, the overall effect is much more educational than promotional.

Ortho provides tremendous self-serve information opportunities to customers of that brand, as the Ortho Problem Solver mobile application enables users to find recommendations customized to their current location. Here in Bloomington, Indiana, I evidently should be concerned about thirty-three types of broadleaf weeds, including the insidious white Dutch clover. For each potential issue—which also includes pests such as mice, ants, and lawn grubs—the Ortho Problem Solver app provides a description, seasonal circumstances, and possible remediation steps. Agrarian hypochondriacs should think

twice before downloading it, as you have nightmares about weevils and dandelions. The app also allows customers to take a photo of a lawn or pest issue and upload it to Ortho help desk personnel.

With more than seven hundred thousand customers, the Scotts Lawn Services division knows a lot about grass, and successfully imparting that knowledge to consumers makes a meaningful difference in company results, according to Beth Dockins, director of Customer Service at Scotts Miracle-Gro.[20]

In many parts of the country lawns are aerated in the spring or fall, depending on grass type. This process creates hundreds or thousands of tiny holes in the turf, allowing oxygen to better circulate under the surface, and enabling fertilizer to penetrate more deeply into the soil. Many experts, including those at Scotts, claim aeration is one of the keys to a healthy lawn. The aftermath of aeration, however, can be pretty ugly, and customers not familiar with the process can be shocked and dismayed, thinking their lawn has been ruined. Dockins says Scotts Lawn Services has produced many videos demonstrating the aeration process, and e-mails to them during aeration season to avoid misunderstandings and surprises. This type of seasonal education makes good business sense, too. According to Dockins, the average customer service phone call costs the company six dollars to field. Every call that is avoided through videos, answering customer questions on Facebook—where the company maintains a two-hour response time—or through the forthcoming new mobile app, saves Scotts Lawn Services several dollars.

"We're very enthusiastic about the new mobile app, and it's particularly relevant for our customers," says Dockins. "We're trying to help you create an experience on your lawn, and if you have a question or concern it's much easier to work on that through a mobile application than it is to lug your laptop outside," she says.

To maintain optimal results, the Lawn Services division asks customers to water and mow to precise specifications provided by the company based on grass type and region. To help consumers better adhere to these guidelines, the new mobile application will have a built-in ruler to help measure mowing height, and the company provides free water depth gauges to all customers.

"We test and measure this all the time," says Dockins. "And the customers that interact with us and our information online or through mobile apps have greater loyalty to

Scotts, and are more likely to promote us to their friends and
family members."

Syncapse Helps Businesses Plan Their Annual Facebook Advertising Budget

Capitalizing on seasonal creation of marketing budgets for
the following year, Syncapse created an online Facebook Advertising Spend Calculator (ar.gy/syncapse) and launched it
in September 2012. A technology company that helps large
business-to-consumer marketers understand and optimize
their social media, Syncapse is trying to get companies to
think about social media (especially social advertising) as an
annual program, rather than a series of short-term campaigns.

Users of this free tool answer a series of questions about
their businesses, their objectives, and their use of Facebook,
and the tool scans their Facebook page in real time, providing a recommended annual budget for Facebook advertising
for the following year.

As companies continue to expand their social media participation, two big questions become important, according
to Max Kalehoff, the vice president of Product Marketing at
Syncapse. The first is "What's the ROI of what you've already
invested in?" Then, secondly, "What decisions are you going
to make differently in the future?" Kalehoff says the Facebook
Advertising Spend Calculator helps answer those questions.[21]

"What we've done with the Facebook Ads Calculator is
provide a very easy, nearly spoon-fed methodology for sur-
facing the most important questions about your brand and
about its situation in the marketplace, in order to extract the
strengths of Facebook," says Kalehoff.

BETA

2013 Facebook Advertising Spend Calculator

In five minutes, you'll know how to establish and allocate your Facebook Ads budget to maximize your specific branding goals.

As Featured In Mashable

Get Started:

Enter Your Facebook Page Url*   https://www.facebook.com/

First Name*   e.g. John

Last Name*

Work Email*   e.g. John@yourcompany.com

☑ Receive Syncapse Social Updates

Calculate

Before you spend a single penny on Facebook ads in 2013, take five minutes to get great planning insights

"As one of the first tools of its kind online, the calculator is being used often, spreading throughout organizations, with multiple people kicking the data tires. They'll put in various parameters and then they'll run it several more times, changing the parameters, and then within the next twenty-four hours you'll see anywhere from two to ten of their colleagues come back on the site," Kalehoff asserts. "It'll help you contextualize and have a reference point for budgeting if you're looking to see how much money of your total pie you should allocate to social media. We're really hoping to sort of stretch the thinking of what's possible."

Syncapse is just one of the companies stretching the thinking of what's possible. Dan Deacon is doing it. So is Vanderbilt. And Clorox. And Charmin. And Taxi Mike. And River

Pools and Spas. With them, we've looked at the three ways to build Youtility: by providing self-serve information, by answering every question, and by being relevant in real time. We know what Youtility is, and how companies are focusing on help, not hype. In the last section of this book you'll learn the six-step process for how you can create your own Youtility.

PART III

Six Blueprints
to Create Youtility

CHAPTER 7
Identify Customer Needs

F or your marketing to be so useful that people want it and would gladly pay for it, you have to understand what your prospective customers need to make better decisions, and how you can improve their lives by providing it. Aided by top-of-mind awareness strategies and a far simpler media marketplace, companies could historically rely on relatively broad customer characterizations to target their marketing and their message. There was a time when trying to reach "twenty-five- to forty-four-year-old housewives in the midwestern United States" qualified as a highly segmented effort. Today, in the age of self-serve information, the demographics of prospective customers are simply the starting point, not the end.

You must align what you provide your customers and prospects with what they actually need. Charmin's Sit or

Squat makes sense and is useful because it answers a specific and important question about restroom cleanliness and reliability. But the insight they tapped to make their marketing useful wasn't just that consumers need to know where to go, but that consumers themselves would review restrooms, thus creating a database to benefit all.

Lee Odden, president of online marketing agency TopRank and author of *Optimize: How to Attract and Engage More Customers by Integrating SEO, Social Media, and Content Marketing*, describes this need to better understand the customer exceptionally well:

"You have to empathize with your target audience in three ways," says Odden. "One, 'How is it that they discover information?' Two, 'What are their preferences for consumption?,' which drills down into channels, and devices and content types. Then the third thing is 'What motivates them to take action?'"[1]

Fortunately, as knowing more about your customers has increased in importance, so has the prevalence of the tools available to gain that understanding. There are a variety of free (or nearly free) approaches that you can use to better understand customer needs on the way to creating Youtility.

Search Engine Data Is the Atlas for Consumer Understanding

While the number of places consumers go to seek information has grown exponentially, weakening somewhat the role of search engines in the process, search engines (especially Google) are unmatched in giving us the ability to mine and analyze consumer-inquiry data.

A variety of free tools from Google can help you understand customer needs, based on what people are looking for, and when. Google Trends (google.com/trends) enables you to compare search volume patterns across location and time frame, and provides related search terms and comparative volume for them.

For example, if you were Sterling Ball from Big Poppa Smokers and thinking about starting a new online forum dedicated to a method of outdoor cooking growing in popularity, an analysis of "pellet smokers" on Google Trends shows a sharp spike in searches for that term in the United States from 2008 onward.[2] Digging deeper, Google Trends shows that Texas and California have disproportionately high incidences of search volume for "pellet smokers," and that "pellet grills smokers" and "Traeger smokers" (a popular brand) are related queries used by searchers.

An even simpler tool is Google Suggest, which can be used to better understand how consumers see your products and services. Type a company or product name into Google and

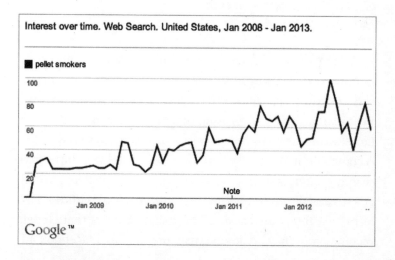

Interest over time. Web Search. United States, Jan 2008 - Jan 2013.

see what Google "suggests" as possible searches. Typing in "Charmin" for example, finds these suggestions: "charmin coupons," "charmin mega roll," and "charmin toilet paper," as well as something called "charming charlie."

This information is updated instantly and is useful for understanding who consumers think your competitors are, and how you stack up. "Type in your company or product name, then put the word 'versus' in and take your hands off the keyboard," recommends Google's Jim Lecinski. "Because brand managers always think they know what the evoked set or the competitive set is because, 'We've done twenty focus groups all across the country . . .' Well, that's cool but let's see what Google says based on actual queries that people are actually comparing you against," he says.

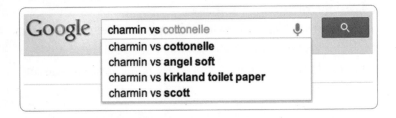

A long-standing favorite of the inbound marketing community, Google's Keyword Tool (googlekeywordtool.com) is often used to determine which search terms to include in a paid search engine advertising campaign. Starting with one, a handful, or hundreds of seed terms, the keyword tool will then recommend a swath of alternatives and display comparative search volume and level of competition (number of existing advertisers per term). Using the Keyword Tool with the seed term "Facebook advertising," for example, finds that Google recommends "facebook advertising cost," "free facebook advertising," "facebook advertisement," "facebook advertising statistics," and "facebook and advertising" as the top five alternatives based on relevance,[3] and "facebook advertising costs" is shown with 8,100 monthly searches on average by consumers, with a high level of competition. In addition to Google's free tool, there are a number of other keyword tools available, including some that are more sophisticated and detailed. An excellent blog post from Arnie Kuenn, president of interactive marketing firm Vertical Measures, provides twelve alternatives to consider (ar.gy/contentresearch).

Google Correlate (google.com/trends/correlate) is the newest of the free Google tools, and it is essentially Google Trends in reverse. The tool allows you to research a term and see what other searches were being performed with similar volume at a similar point in time, or in the same regions. It's outstanding when used to uncover seasonal and location-specific inquiry patterns. For example, Google Correlate shows that the search term "pellet smokers" has a .8947 correlation with the search term "big 12 basketball standings"[4] across the entire country, but the correlation in Kansas (where two of the Big 12 members' universities are located) has a correlation of 4.814. If Big Poppa Smokers wants to find a way to provide exceptionally useful marketing for its customers in Kansas (and throughout the Big 12 region), a program that sends text messages with instant basketball score updates might make for a successful implementation.

Mike Corak, executive vice president at interactive marketing agency Ethology and a board member of the Search Engine Marketers Professional Organization, says using search data to determine where a company can be helpful is a difficult but necessary process:

"It's hard work. It's elbow grease, but that's what a lot

of people aren't willing to do, to dig into it and find the opportunities that come when you outhustle the competition,"[5] says Corak. "We start with the broad 'trail head' topics and then dig into the 'long tail'[6] around them, and we're letting the public speak from a popularity standpoint."

Social Chatter Uncovers Customer Needs

Nothing reveals real-time customer queries like social media. In my first book, *The NOW Revolution*, I wrote about the "anyone know" phenomenon in social media, particularly Twitter. Every second of every day consumers are seeking answers and solutions, often phrasing those queries as "Anyone know . . ." Go to Twitter and type "Anyone know" into the search box right now, and you'll see a river of inquiry flowing by.

In practice, that type of research is better suited for companies looking to provide solutions at the point of need, which is one form of Youtility (@HiltonSuggests does this, for instance). However, for most companies looking to make their marketing more useful, examining social chatter more broadly will be a better way to surface consumer desires. Most midsized and larger companies, especially those in business-to-consumer environments, use social media "listening" and analysis tools on a regular basis. But, as Corak notes, these tools are used for narrow, brand-focused research. "Most companies that have a social monitoring tool are almost always using it for brand listening, and for brand sentiment analysis,[7] and they are getting pretty good at that," Corak says. "But it's very rare for us to see somebody doing a great job of listening around the broader topics that impact the company and its customers."

This is the difference between using social listening tools like Marketing Cloud from Salesforce (radian6.com) or Sysomos (sysomos.com) or Viralheat (viralheat.com) to search for "Clorox" versus searching for all social conversations about stain removal and remedies. Netbase (netbase.com) is a software tool that specializes in uncovering these broader customer insights that can assist with product development and Youtility. Netbase uses natural language processing to examine all social conversations around a brand or category, and then isolates nuggets of insight that may not be noticed while using other tools or more specific searches. An e-book I wrote with Netbase in 2012 called *Knockout! Using Conversation Mining and Facebook Data to Thump Your Competition* (ar.gy/knockout) includes an example of this difference. Looking at social media chatter around the Corvette brand finds a steady level of conversations, almost all of which are positive. A Netbase examination of Corvette conversations on Facebook uncovered that many of them are rooted in nostalgia, with a particular connection to fathers. In theory, this insight, combined with search engine data and other sources, might cause Corvette to consider creating Youtility centered on Father's Day.

This type of social media insight is an excellent cross-reference for search-driven research.

Web Analytics and Internal Search Show You What's Working Today

Even if your website only includes twenty pages, like Marcus Sheridan's River Pools and Spas site before he began answering customer questions, the pages that are popular among your visitors can help you better understand what customers want from you. If particular pages or elements of your site (such as Holiday World's ride descriptions) are getting a disproportionately large share of visitor attention, that's a signal that you should consider expanding information of that type. Also look at the differences between what visitors to your site from mobile devices are seeking versus visitors from computers. Mobile users are typically seeking a very specific answer, or are attempting to engage in a particular behavior or transaction. They are purposeful website visitors. Given the increase in smartphone adoption, pay particular attention to how this audience engages with you online, as they are the advance guard for how most people will eventually behave.

Another illuminating, yet mostly overlooked, stream of data is the internal search report. This shows what website visitors are typing into the search box located on your website, if you have one. This is very useful information, as it shows precisely what people wanted from your site but were unable to find on their own without searching.

All of this data is available in website analytics software, including Google Analytics (google.com/analytics), Adobe Site Catalyst (adobe.com/sitecatalyst), Webtrends (webtrends.com), HubSpot (hubspot.com), KISSmetrics (kissmetrics.com), and others. But availability doesn't equal usage. The fragmentation of marketing and the explosion of new channels of communication makes getting a holistic analytics picture difficult for nonspecialists. "Not only are companies not doing customer research in terms of surveys or focus groups, but a lot of companies aren't really even digging into the data that they're sitting on," says Lee Odden. "They're sitting on gold mines of data about their customers, and I don't even mean the 'big data' stuff, but just website analytics and social monitoring, let alone transaction and conversion data. They just aren't doing nearly as much as they could be."[8]

Ask Your Customers What They Want

A few years ago, I did some consulting for Claire Burke, a company that manufactures and sells a range of candles and scented air fresheners. Distributed in department stores, gift shops, and on their own website, Claire Burke products were primarily purchased by women thirty-five to fifty-four years old. Research told us this, and it was interesting information that we used when purchasing different forms of media to communicate to that segment of the population. But, knowing that thirty-five- to fifty-four-year-old women buy your products isn't particularly helpful in this age of information. Demographics provide the "who" but fall far short of "what" and "why." Knowing what your customers need to know and why they purchase from you is absolutely critical to successful Youtility.

An effort led by my friend Susan Baier, a brilliant marketer who now has her own customer segmentation research company called Audience Audit, dug deeper into the motivations behind Claire Burke purchases. Of the five segments identified in the research, one group (approximately 15 percent) of customers purchased Claire Burke candles primarily because of the fragrance—the motivation the company was most familiar with. However, two other groups bought them for very different reasons: Twenty-five percent bought the candles to decorate their homes, so color and design were more important to them than fragrance, and 21 percent purchased them primarily as gifts, and cared more about the upscale brand and packaging. Customers were indeed most likely to be thirty-five- to fifty-four-year-old females, but their rationale for purchasing the products fell into three highly specific, wholly disparate segments. The more you know about your customers and prospects, the more useful your brand can become to them.

Beyond the computer-aided research tools discussed in this chapter, the single best way to understand what your customers need is to ask them. Customer segmentation analysis of the type Baier and others provide is an excellent approach, but even unstructured, nonscientific conversations can yield outstanding results.

For example, the CoachSmart app was guided significantly by feedback Nashville-area coaches gave trainers from Vanderbilt Medical Center. "We sent our trainers out to talk to the coaches they work with and asked, 'how would an app make your coaching life a little bit easier and keep the kids safer?' and the number one thing that came back was lightning," says Betsy Brandes from Vanderbilt. "We had already built the heat index function, but we met with our trainers and they had lots of ideas. Lightning was one we thought we could probably do."[9]

Sitting down in a conference room with an agenda item of "let's be useful" is 100 percent the wrong way to change your marketing mindset. True Youtility requires more understanding of the lives, desires, and fears of your customers and prospects than ever. Creating marketing so useful that people would pay for it isn't a proactive exercise, it's a reactive one. First, identify the problem, then find a way for your company to remove that problem.

Look at how easy it is to understand the problems addressed by companies profiled in this book so far:

GEEK SQUAD: "How do I fix <electronic thing>?"

HILTON SUGGESTS: "Anyone know <local recommendation>?"

PHOENIX CHILDREN'S HOSPITAL: "How do I know which car seat to buy?"

CHARMIN: "Where should I go to go?"

TAXI MIKE: "Where should I eat in Banff?"

LIFE TECHNOLOGIES: "Which of your products is right for me?"

CLOROX: "How do I remove this stain?"

BIG POPPA SMOKERS: "Should I buy a pellet smoker? How do I use it?"

ANGIE'S LIST: "Who should I hire for <service>?"

HOLIDAY WORLD: "What's it like at your amusement park?"

MCDONALD'S CANADA: "Is it true that <food question>?"

WARBY PARKER: "What would I look like in new glasses?"

FREEZER BURNS: "Should I buy <frozen food>?"

MEIJER: "How can I make this shopping trip as fast as possible?"

VANDERBILT: "Should we continue practice or cancel it?"

DAN DEACON: "How can I enjoy this concert even more?"

SCOTTS: "What should I do about this <lawn problem>?"

SYNCAPSE: "How much should I spend on Facebook ads next year?"

All of these questions are important to customers, and, without understanding what customers really need and when, none of the Youtility created to satiate those needs could exist. Additionally, without successfully resisting the urge to turn the answers to those questions into an overt sales pitch, none would be successful.

The questions answered by these companies are especially relevant to consumers at certain points in time, which is why mobile is such a big part of many of the successes we've studied. But it's not the only way to do it, and figuring out how to package usefulness is step two in becoming a Youtility.

CHAPTER 8
Map Customer Needs to Useful Marketing

I wasn't much of a Boy Scout. In fact, even though my mom was the "den mother" for most of it, the entirety of my scouting career spanned about three years. I wasn't anti-kerchief per se, but let's just say my career as an avid indoorsman began at an early age. Which is why as a middle-aged adult, I am so delighted to be able to partially compensate for my lack of outdoor aptitude with useful marketing from Columbia Sportswear.

Columbia Sportswear, a Portland, Oregon–based manufacturer and retailer of outdoor wear and gear, has a circumstantially useful free app called "What Knot to Do in the Greater Outdoors." As you've probably guessed, it provides detailed instructions for how to tie dozens of knots, including which to use when. The app has the best ratings of any mentioned in this book, with forty-eight five-star reviews out

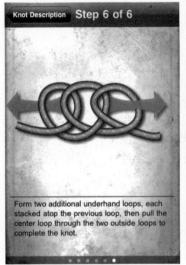

Knot Description   Step 6 of 6

Form two additional underhand loops, each stacked atop the previous loop, then pull the center loop through the two outside loops to complete the knot.

Knot Categories   Knot Description

Category: Bends   ABOK: #1463
Heaving Line Bend

Similar to a Sheet Bend, but more secure, the Heaving Line Bend works well with lines that differ greatly in diameter. That is, when one line is fatter than the other.

Use this bend to attach a light messenger line to a heavy hawser.

Step-by-step   Add to Favorites

of fifty-three total reviews in the Apple iTunes Store.[1] With little marketing support, it's been downloaded 351,000 times in approximately twenty months.

According to Adam Buchanan, formerly the social media manager at Columbia, the company conducted research and found it is very common for outdoor enthusiasts to carry smartphones on excursions. "Customers regularly report using the camera, GPS, and music features of their devices while in the field, in addition to its obvious use as a phone," he says.[2]

It makes perfect sense. If you need to remember how to tie a knot, being able to recall that information with the assistance of a mobile device is far more practical and reasonable than accessing that information through other methods. It's similar to the Ortho pests app in that mobile is the most appropriate venue for that particular Youtility.

But what form your helpfulness should take isn't always as obvious and tidy. One of the most difficult aspects of this type of marketing is effectively and appropriately translating customer needs into actual executions. Part of the problem is that many companies get excited and jump the gun, coupling customer questions uncovered via the tactics discussed in the last chapter with the formats in which those questions will get answered. Instead of saying "we need to help customers figure out this problem," they go further and say, "we need a blog to help customers figure out this problem." This combines the symptom and the cure, and can yield disappointing results.

Robert Rose, content strategist in residence for the Content Marketing Institute and coauthor of *Managing Content Marketing*, says decoupling these questions is all-important:

"You start with the story, and then you figure out what the best mechanism for telling it is," he says.[3] "Going way back to my own storytelling days, my writing instructors would say to me, 'When you write a story, it will either be a play, a screenplay, a television show, or a novel. It won't be all of those things. It cannot be.'"

The same is true of Youtility. Determining the optimal conveyance mechanism requires a level of research beyond understanding customer needs. You have to understand not just what your customers need, but how and where they prefer to access information. Ann Handley, the chief content officer for the education and training company MarketingProfs, believes there is no substitute for customer research in this part of the planning process. "Ask them 'What do you read?' 'How do you consume content?' 'Are you even online, and if so where are you?' 'What publications do you read in what format?'"[4] Handley says many businesses focus on determining customer needs at the exclusion of determining this critical second half of the success equation. "A lot of companies survey their customers and find out what their pain points are, and they get a sense of what they should be creating content about. Often they don't think about, 'Well, how are they consuming content, and how do they like to be communicated with?'"

In some cases there aren't right and wrong answers to the question of how to address customer needs; there are just answers that are more right versus more wrong. Consider the Phoenix Children's Hospital Car Seat Helper app discussed in chapter 3. The customer need is: "How do I know which car seat to buy?" That need could be fulfilled in many ways. PCH could have created a series of blog posts about car seats. They could have created an ongoing series of videos, like Greg Ng's *Freezer Burns*. They could have created a downloadable e-book about car seat models and advice. They could have created a physical book, giving it to local pediatricians' offices to distribute to parents. They could have conducted a series of events at the hospital where employees would work with parents one-on-one to answer car seat questions, making sure the seats were correctly installed. All of these could have worked. But they chose to create a mobile application because they determined that young parents who have their own automobiles are more likely to have smartphones than other audiences, and the information would be particularly useful for them to access while in a retail environment.

The event-based alternative is particularly interesting, as there are circumstances in which face-to-face Youtility is ideal, even in this self-serve information era. In the days following Superstorm Sandy, Duracell batteries took usefulness to the streets. The company sent its Power Forward Community Center and Rapid Responder off-road-capable truck to lower Manhattan, where power outages persisted for days.

Both are equipped with charging stations for mobile phones and include onboard computers with built-in Internet access, enabling people affected by the natural disaster to use their e-mail and social media. "This is what the brand is about," says Will Sakdinan, spokesman for Duracell, "empowering people through devices; connecting their families."[5]

Atomize Your Marketing to Reach a Larger Audience

While Robert Rose and his storytelling instructors are right that there is an optimal format for every story, they are perhaps being too strident in suggesting that there is only one way to answer every question. There are certainly programs that are a poor fit for audiences. Mobile apps, for example, are probably not the best option for reaching seniors yet. But, in many instances, it's not only possible to create Youtility in several formats, but doing so can also increase efficiency and exposure. In the excellent book *Content Rules*, coauthored with C. C. Chapman, Ann Handley writes about taking one big idea or customer need and creating multiple executions out of it.

"We recommend that businesses reimagine their content, but that they don't recycle it," says Handley. "It's not about taking a blog post and just putting it on Pinterest and on Facebook and on LinkedIn. You're just filling links that way. It's important to reimagine it completely. Take something and create something new out of it."[6]

Todd Defren, of the public relations firm Shift Communications, calls this premise "atomizing" your marketing. Not only does creating more variations of your usefulness help reach customers with a variety of information consumption habits (Phoenix Children's Hospital could create the mobile app *and* a blog *and* an event, for example), but this type of diffuse approach can more effectively and strategically target prospects in different stages of the research process.

The excellent online presentation "From Content to Customer" (ar.gy/content2customer), published in 2011 by the marketing automation software company Eloqua, divides the prospective customer pool into three distinct groups: Suspects, Prospects, Leads, and Opportunities, and suggests that certain information packages are more likely to be consumed by each, especially in a business-to-business scenario.

Suspects are the broadest audience with nearly no understanding of your company and its offerings. Suspects want to know what your company knows, not what you sell. This is where blogs like Marcus Sheridan's for River Pools and Spas can be a tremendous difference maker. Eloqua also recommends infographics, videos, and "infotainment" for Suspects.

Prospects are defined as having supplied personal data in exchange for more information. The requirement in the Sit or Squat app to connect via Facebook makes its users Prospects, based on the Eloqua framework. Prospects want information that relates to their particular interests. The Scotts Lawn Care Update e-mail is an excellent example of the formats favored by Prospects. Other options include direct mail, events, online webinars, reports, and guides.

A Lead is a Prospect who meets specific, predetermined criteria making them disproportionately likely to become a customer. Leads desire specific information addressing their circumstances. The Life Sciences interactive video product finder is a good example of the Youtility favored by this audience. Other formats to consider include white papers, product comparisons, and one-on-one help, such as being able to take a photo and send it to Ortho.

Opportunities are potential customers who are ready to buy. This is when Prospects cross the chasm from self-serve to full-serve. This is when personalized relationship building takes over the process. In short, this is when marketing yields sales. Marcus Sheridan writing blog posts reaches Suspects. Marcus Sheridan showing up in your living room to talk about swimming pools is all about Opportunities.

Smart companies take their core informational value proposition and package it in ways that appeal to more than one of these prospective customer segments, or even all four. Handley particularly appreciates the recent efforts of the global technology company Cisco in this area. The company's 2011 Global Cloud Index report forecasts data center and cloud computing traffic and related trends for 2011 through 2016, and highlights workload transitions from traditional information technology (IT) to cloud solutions as well.[7] It is not light reading. But Cisco didn't just create this massive report, release it, and say "we hope you like it." They were smart enough to create a spoonful of sugar to help the informational medicine go down. "They took a giant report and made it inherently more consumable and interesting for the customer. They created a supershort, one-and-a-half-minute video (ar.gy/cisco) to describe how big cloud computing will be. It distills the essence of this report into something that's fun and accessible and engaging," says Handley.[8]

Regardless of how many times you reimagine the ways you can fulfill customer and prospective customer needs, remember that to be a true Youtility, this fulfillment must be free. Friend-of-mine awareness is predicated on the principle that, if you are useful without engaging in an immediate quid pro-quo, your business will be trusted the same way consumers trust their friends and family members. When you tilt toward promotion and away from information, that trust evaporates. And, says Joe Chernov, vice president of marketing for the mobile technology provider Kinvey (and 2012's Content Marketing Visionary of the Year by the Content Marketing Institute), keeping your marketing free increases its exposure. "If you create something that somebody would pay for, but you give it away, not only are you building trust and a debt of gratitude but you shock them into sharing it," says Chernov. "They share not only the asset itself, which is inherently valuable to the brand, but they share the fact that they are surprised that a brand would just give it to them and not try to sell them along the way."[9]

Understanding what people need to know from you is only half the battle. You also have to know how they consume information and the best way (or ways) to execute your useful marketing. Next we'll discover another critically important blueprint to create Youtility: making sure your customers and prospects know what you've made.

CHAPTER 9
Market Your Marketing

You know what happens when most companies launch a new, branded mobile application or other content-rich marketing program intended to effectively combine information and promotion? Nothing. You've heard the saying "If a tree falls in the forest, and no one is around to hear it, does it make a sound?" The same logic works in these scenarios: "If you create Youtility and don't tell anyone about it, does it even exist?"

When you launch the app, or commence blogging, or begin answering questions, you have not reached the finish line; you have reached the starting line. Too many businesses break out the champagne just because something new was created. Remember, Youtility is all about being useful, which literally means "full of use." The objective is not to make information. The objective is to make information that customers and prospective customers will use.

However, because creating Youtility is often an inexpensive proposition when considered in the context of the overall marketing program of a company, these efforts are viewed as relatively minor and thus don't receive dedicated promotional support, even at launch. Instead, they are promoted alongside the regular flotsam and jetsam of the brand's communication: a link here, a mention there. This not only dramatically curtails exposure—counteracting the entire premise of the Youtility—but wastes an opportunity for the company to combine top-of-mind awareness and friend-of-mine awareness in interesting, evocative ways.

"I bought a bag of toilet paper at Safeway or Costco, and in the bag was this little thing from Charmin that said, 'Fill out this form and send it in for a thirty-five-cent coupon," says Avinash Kaushik, author of *Web Analytics 2.0* and the digital marketing evangelist at Google. "Really?" Why doesn't it say, 'Did you know we have an amazing mobile app called Sit or Squat?'"[1]

He's right. If you believe in your ability to sell more by selling less, and if you're committed to creating truly helpful information that will add value to the lives of your customers and prospective customers, you also have to add the third leg of the stool. You have to market your marketing.

The Phoenix Children's Hospital Car Seat Helper app had a dedicated marketing plan designed to create awareness and downloads among the target audience of parents of young children in metropolitan Phoenix. The marketing plan covered thirty days post launch and was created approximately sixty days before the app was finished, according to Allison Otu, the former Media Relations Specialist for the hospital.[2]

The marketing plan for the app included these elements:

- Promotion on website home page
- Promotion on the hospital's social media outlets
- Inclusion in e-mail newsletter sent to eleven thousand supporters
- E-mail sent to all employees
- Working with local media partners to demonstrate the app on several local television morning shows and radio programs
- National media program that secured placements in parenting and health magazines

Brian Berg from MediaKube, who developed the app, also created a demonstration video for YouTube to describe the features and ease of using of the Car Seat helper (ar.gy/carseat). And it's not as though PCH has the luxury of unlimited marketing resources. Otu was one half of a two-person media relations team supporting four thousand employees and one thousand physicians in fifty subspecialties.

C. C. Chapman, coauthor of *Content Rules*, is a fervent believer in the need to market your marketing. "The first step is the research of figuring out your audience," he says. "Then, part two is having something interesting that they'll care about. But the third step is a whole separate strategy to get people to find it. It's almost like people skip over that step and just jump right to 'We're going to create this really cool thing and put it out there and people are going to magically find it.'"[3]

Beyond creating a sound plan with tangible support, a specific tactic to market your marketing is to use hypertargeting to boost circumstantial relevance. Local Response (localresponse. com) is a mobile advertising network that enables brands to target advertising based on location, mobile operating system, and content posted to social media. Called "intent targeting," this would allow Phoenix Children's Hospital to show a mobile ad only to people in Arizona with smartphones who have mentioned "car seat" on Twitter or Facebook, for example.

Another interesting option is using on-the-fly website ingredient swapping to promote Youtility components to website visitors. Insightera (insightera.com), a real-time content marketing software company from Israel, licenses a system that allows companies to dynamically and automatically change blog posts, case studies, photos, videos, and other components of the website based on visitors' locations, keyword use (when coming from search), and past on-site behavior. For instance, Geek Squad could recommend specific videos to website visitors automatically, based on which products they've purchased on BestBuy.com.

This concept of using marketing to promote your marketing is also the best possible case for using social media, which far too often devolves into self-referential inanities that career employees wouldn't even care about, much less casual customers. This frustrating scenario of brands talking, talking, talking in social media but never saying anything of value other than "we're great, you should give us more of your money" is the epitome of the Caveman 2.0 syndrome we examined in Part 1.

Marketing humorist Tom Fishburne captures this reality perfectly in his brilliant "5 Types of Social Media Strategies" cartoon:

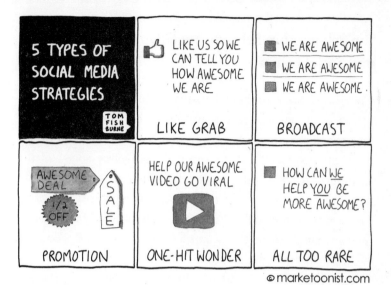

© marketoonist.com

"How can *we* help *you* be more awesome?" is indeed a worthy rallying cry, and the most straightforward way to meet that challenge is to promote your information more while promoting your company less. On the whole, which is more inherently interesting and useful, and thus more likely to be an effective marketing message: That Columbia Sportswear sells a variety of outdoor gear, or that Columbia Sportswear has a mobile app that shows you how to tie knots? Remember, companies of every size, shape, and description are competing for attention with real people whom we know and love. It's not about keeping it real; it's about keeping it relevant. If your social media informs more often than it promotes, you're on the right track.

• • •

The Relationship Between Youtility and Social Media

Content is fire, and social media is gasoline. Utilize social media to create awareness and usage of your Youtility. Interactive marketing software company ExactTarget does this from time to time, but it cannot devote every social media communication to information (and neither can your company). Because there are, of course, other priorities fighting for attention internally. But being useful and interesting and relevant needs to be the least of what your brand is known for, now and into the future.

The Coca-Cola Company has embraced this principle fully, producing two videos in 2011 (ar.gy/CocaCola1 and ar.gy/CocaCola2) that set forth their global strategy for using content as a strategic scaffold for everything and everywhere the company communicates.

The architect of their new approach is Jonathan Mildenhall, vice president of Global Advertising Strategy and Creative Excellence. Interviewed by Robert Rose of the Content Marketing Institute for a blog post about the initiative,[4] Mildenhall describes the intersection of promotional and informational messaging. "We fully understand that we are still going to have to do promotions, price messaging, shopper bundles, traditional advertising, et cetera—that isn't going away. But content is the way consumers understand the role and relevance of the Coca-Cola Company brands. We have to make sure that those 'immediate stories' are part of the larger brand stories," Mildenhall says. "But, for the more financially minded in our organization, I say this: 'If

I can fill up the emotional level of the brand, then I have to trade on it less and less.'"

Precisely. If you're interesting and useful and helpful, your customers and prospects will do more of your marketing for you, helping your company work less arduously and expensively on interruption marketing in its various guises.

Here's a real example of this confluence, featuring back-to-back messages sent by interactive marketing software company ExactTarget on their Twitter channel in July 2012:

ExactTarget @ExactTarget
Hallo! Olá! We've launched our enterprise marketing platform in German & Brazilian Portuguese! Learn more: bit.ly/OJHYNa

ExactTarget @ExactTarget
Facts and Figures Behind Social Media & the Olympics #exacttarget #Infographic bit.ly/OIHD30

The first tweet is a mundane corporate message about a new version of the company's software, made even less powerful because it's only relevant to persons seeking a German or Brazilian Portuguese version of the software—presumably a small subset of the brand's followers on Twitter.

In the very next tweet, ExactTarget gets it entirely right. Sent during the London Olympic Games, the message includes a link that, when clicked, accesses a very interesting infographic, showing which Olympic sports have the most tweets about them, the most followers on Twitter, and several other statistical tidbits.

Does the infographic explicitly provide information about ExactTarget's products and services? It does not. Instead it uses the real-time relevancy approach discussed in Chapter 6.

The Most Popular Olympic Sports Based on Followers

It should be **noted** that these numbers were recorded **June 5-12, 2012** and will likely see boosts closer to and during the Olympics. This is especially true as narratives develop and people decide to tune in to sports they don't normally watch, as occurred previously with Michael Phelps and Shawn Johnson.
*Each sport and number represents the official London Olympics Twitter handle for each sport and number of followers.

Equestrian	Swimming	Volleyball
1025	1021	845

Road Cycle	Athletics	Badminton	Tae Kwon Do	Track Cycle	Triathlon	Boxing	Handball	Judo
729	728	680	676	560	524	516	486	483

Diving	475	Synchro Swim	286
Football	469	Beach Volleyball	285
Archery	437	Weightlifting	261
Artistic Gym	389	Water Polo	260
Sailing	388	Table Tennis	260
Rowing	386	Canoe Sprint	255
Mountain Bike	364	Shooting	236
Wrestling	352	Trampoline	230
Basketball	335	Canoe Slalom	229
Hockey	334	Mod Penathlon	210
BMX	303	Fencing	178
Rhythmic Gym	294		

Most Popular Olympic Athletes   Social Media x Medal Ratio

There is an implied topical tie, however, as one of the company's products is software that allows companies to monitor and engage on Twitter.

Using marketing to promote your information assets isn't solely an online tactic, either. Angie's List publishes a monthly magazine in print and online that cannily underscores the value of membership with feature articles like "Winter Weather Sends Mice and Rats Indoors" and "Electricians Recommend GFCI Outlets for Holiday Lights." One of the most useful—and most read—elements of the magazine is the "Penalty Box," where the Angie's List editorial team spotlights under-performing service providers and common scams and rip-offs, which makes it abundantly clear that Angie's List is on the side of the consumer. The magazine is no minor afterthought to the company, as the publication won fifteen awards for graphic design and editorial excellence in 2011 alone. It's an integral part of the company's overall focus on being helpful. The magazine "has simply grown with us along the way," says Cheryl Reed from Angie's List. "It's gotten better, and it's gotten more sophisticated since the days that Angie herself was the editor and reporter, but we've had the magazine all along. It's just another way to get our messaging in front of people and to prod that interaction with us."[5]

Another way Angie's List is wise about marketing their marketing is with their member survey. Each year, the company asks members what household project they are considering for the coming twelve months. This is not only an excellent way to better understand customer needs to build Youtility around them, but it's a cagey public relations program, too. The company releases the consolidated, consensus results of their survey, and partners with nearly seventy television stations throughout the United States who feature the information on a weekly segment.

Your Most Important (and Most Often Overlooked) Audience

Indeed, you should use online and offline tactics to raise awareness of the truly helpful information you're providing to customers and prospective customers, and smart organizations like Phoenix Children's Hospital and Angie's List are successfully implementing those ideas. But there is another critically important audience for your Youtility that is consistently overlooked—your employees. If you are truly, inherently useful, the manifestation of that approach will be just as valuable to your team members as it is to customers, maybe even more so. You know who is particularly interested in an application that shows you how to tie knots? People who work for Columbia Sportswear. Many are outdoors enthusiasts and are disproportionately likely to find themselves in a situation that calls for just the right knot. In addition to the fact that they are likely to enjoy and benefit from your Youtility, there is one big reason you should make employees a key target audience.

In a world where personal relationships and social connectivity are the coin of the realm, your employees are your single greatest marketing engine. With the exception of huge, global consumer brands like Coca-Cola, the collected social connections of your employees exceed the social connections of your company, and those employees are perfectly situated to create awareness of your helpful marketing.

Look at ExactTarget. As of December 2012, the company had approximately 37,000 social connections across its official Facebook and Twitter presences.[6] There is no doubt some overlap between those networks, and some of those 37,000 connections are employees, but let's just assume it does represent 37,000 unique connections with customers, prospective customers, and other interested parties (media, analysts, competitors, et al). ExactTarget currently has 1,352 employees.[7] Because it is an interactive marketing company that sells social media software (among other offerings), the overwhelming majority of those employees are likely active on Facebook or Twitter in some fashion. But, let's use Edison Research's finding in the 2012 Social Habit survey that found that 54 percent of Americans have a Facebook account, and 10 percent have a Twitter account.[8] Let's also use research from the Pew Research Center in 2012 showing the average Facebook user with 229 connections,[9] and a 2012 survey from Beevolve pegging the average number of Twitter followers at 208 per user.[10] A subsequent calculation of $(1,352 \times 0.54 \times 229) + (1,352 \times 0.10 \times 208)$ finds that ExactTarget employees have an estimated 194,579 connections across Facebook and Twitter. The size of the employee network is more than five times greater than the company network.

Remember that businesses are now being forced to compete for attention, line by line and pixel by pixel, with our best friends and closest family members. This is the fundamental trend that powers friend-of-mine awareness and the rise of Youtility as an umbrella marketing approach. Thus, if you're setting out to market your marketing, you have no better conduit than your employees, who can reach customers and prospects on the individual, person-to-person basis that is at the core of all modern social technology. Today, every employee is in marketing. Having an active and informed team gives your business far more opportunities to engage and create awareness of your information.

IBM gave a presentation to the Word of Mouth Marketing Association (WOMMA) conference in Fall 2012 (ar.gy/ IBMinfluence) about their employee social activation program and, in one slide, underscored their commitment to this principle. "At IBM, we must shift our focus from large campaigns to one-to-one, high-value interactions," the slide read. "From controlling the message to building collaborative relationships. From being generally accessible to being in the right places at the right times."

ExactTarget has an ongoing series of helpful research called Subscribers, Fans and Followers (ar.gy/sffresearch). It's a multi-part research project that helps companies understand trends in social media, e-mail marketing, mobile, and consumer behavior. According to Chief Marketing Officer Tim Kopp, the priority for Subscribers, Fans, and Followers (SFF) isn't just getting it front of prospects, but first getting it in front of employees. "We've had to spend a lot of time not just launching SFF, but backing up and spending time on 'How do we train our sales team to speak to SFF?' as well as 'How do we get the management team ready to speak to it?'" Kopp says. "We've had to spend equal time capturing the attention of everybody inside the company, as well as everybody outside the company. It's actually a companywide initiative."[11]

Kopp and ExactTarget ignored this internal education and activation step with the first iteration of SFF, and it didn't work. Now, Kopp instructs his content and thought leadership team to be more deliberate. "I said, 'Guys, you've got to slow down, and when you're done, it's not done. When you're done, it means it needs another three weeks, because we have to spend all the internal time educating, enabling, making sure people understand what it is.'"

In *The NOW Revolution*, I wrote about the "Message of the Day" concept, wherein the marketing department would send a message to employees active in social media, recommending messages that team members might want to spread to their own social networks. Imagine Columbia Sportswear e-mailing all employees with a Facebook account, nudging them to inform their connections about the brand-new knot application. When I cowrote that book, I envisioned the "Message of the Day" being pushed via e-mail or an internal social media application like Yammer or Chatter. Since then, however, purpose-built software solutions like Addvocate (addvocate.com) have emerged that give marketers a sound, easy-to-use method for harnessing the remarkable ability of employees to effectively support the company in social media, complete with details such as metrics and analytics.

Already we're seeing companies make hiring decisions based at least in part on employees' social connections. This is the new Rolodex, and it mirrors the way salespeople have used their contacts as a portable, desirable attribute for decades. The social connections of your employees are assets that shouldn't be overlooked, and activating and training employees to be more present and successful on social networks is a fast-growing component of the social business consulting industry.

CHAPTER 10
Insource Youtility

I n business, every important new function starts as a job and eventually becomes a skill. Once we determine that a particular business process is critical, it is decentralized and baked into the day-to-day responsibilities of most employees. This has happened over and over again. Typing used to be a job and companies had entire rooms of people who did nothing but type. It seemed like a terrific notion at the time, but then we decided that typing was sufficiently useful that most everyone should learn how to do it, and so we have. At my very first "real" job, there was a lady who was in charge of the mailroom and making copies. Margie made all copies; doing so yourself was a foolish risk not worth taking. In those days, the copy machine was the size of a small car, noisy and dangerous like mining equipment. Technology improved, and we determined that everyone should be able to make copies themselves. Making copies was a job; now it's a skill.

Social media is moving along the same trajectory. Most companies have historically centralized social media responsibilities in the hands of one person (or at least one department), and now employees are being encouraged to not only advocate on behalf of their employer, as we saw in the last chapter, but to help perpetuate Youtility themselves.

Most organizations that decide to try to win the war of information will put a person or a department in charge of creating helpful content that satisfies the needs of customers and prospects. Don't fall into that trap. Yes, you need someone to oversee and manage your efforts, but creating marketing so useful that people would be willing to pay you for it should be a widely dispersed responsibility. You need to insource your Youtility program because just about every employee has useful knowledge locked in their head. It's time to unlock it.

Not only does involving a wide variety of employees make it easier to create and maintain helpful information, it also increases effectiveness because they bring credibility that centralized, official communication doesn't have.

The 2011 Edelman Trust Barometer found that both company experts (internal thought leaders like Clorox's Dr. Laundry) and regular employees are trusted far more than CEOs, yet most company information is created from the top-down perspective.

Tapping into this well of trust should be a primary objective of all insourced Youtility programs, and there are four ways to get employees involved. In ascending order of rigor, they are: circumstantial participation, voluntary participation, assisted participation, and mandatory participation.

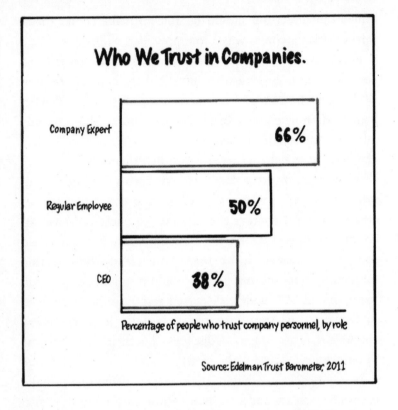

Who We Trust in Companies.

Company Expert — **66%**

Regular Employee — **50%**

CEO — **38%**

Percentage of people who trust company personnel, by role

Source: Edelman Trust Barometer, 2011

They all can work, and, according to Amy Treanor from Edelman, each helps companies make the transition from solely selling products and services to providing information that facilitates the former. "Richard Edelman, our CEO, talks about the need for every company today to be a media company. And, I think that people think of blogs and they think of it as a single voice," she says. "But when you get into the idea of what it means for a company to be a media company, you have to have a bevy of reporters covering all different sorts of specialties. News agencies don't have just one person writing all of their news. You have to have your business and life reporters and you have to have your sports reporter, and

I think the same sort of construct applies to any business out there that is communicating."[1]

She's right. And sometimes, you need a french fries reporter.

McDonald's Canada and Circumstantial Insourcing

The array of inquiries that consumers log on the Our Food, Your Questions website is extremely broad, and this is by design. But, because many of the questions are very specific and involve sourcing and production methods, no single person (or even the twelve-person team that oversees the program) can address them all. That oversight group, called the Conversation Center, fields the questions and answers any that have already been handled in the past. For all others, they develop a knowledge trail to find the answer, involving other McDonald's employees, the supply chain team at the company, and suppliers such as Cargill.

When the circumstances, triggered by a consumer question, call for it, the company taps into the appropriate internal resource, augmented by external suppliers who are working closely with McDonald's on this program.

This process, of course, creates extra work for the supply chain team and suppliers, who have to find answers to questions that may require research, such as this one from Charles S. of Concord, Ontario:

"There is a concern that animals are bred to reach a maximum weight in the shortest time. At what age is your livestock put to slaughter?"

Or from Richie B. in Kitchener, Ontario:

"Does each province have growers for there [sic] potatoes to make there [sic] fries?"

(On the fries question, McDonald's created an excellent and informative five-minute video about their potato supply chain that's been viewed more than two million times on YouTube: ar.gy.mcdonaldsfries.)

"Everyone's excited to spend the time doing it," says Chief Marketing Officer Joel Yashinsky. Our supply chain team, who have had to put in extra hours to help us get those answers to questions . . . You say to them, 'Thank you,' and they're like, 'Listen, for this program, we'll go through the wall.' Because everyone realizes that this is the only way this program is going to work."[2]

SAP and Voluntary Insourcing

Michael Brenner realized SAP had a problem. In his role as senior director for Global Integrated Marketing and Content Strategy, Brenner was analyzing the traffic on the website of the massive, German-based software and services company. He found that just three out of every ten thousand visitors to the site coming from search engines used anything other than the names of the company or its products. The website was solely preaching to the choir (people familiar enough with SAP to look for it by name), leaving a colossal amount of potential attention on the table.

"Think about that," says Brenner. "Think of all the millions of people that don't know us yet. The people that know us are a small percentage. The people that don't know us are the huge percentage. There is a huge audience of businesspeople who know what they want, but don't know that SAP provides it."[3]

Nearly one year later, Brenner and his small team launched the *SAP Business Innovation* blog to answer customer questions, provide helpful information and successfully tie SAP to topics like cloud computing and mobile marketing. At least eight posts are published each day from a rotating, yet still very small, cast of insourced contributors.

"I call it a crusade because, literally, people within the company think I'm crazy for suggesting that we need our entire employee base to be participating in the content development process," he says. "Knowledge, expertise, and passion exist all over the company. But there is in no way a cultural motivation at the company, even in the undertones of our culture, that encourages our people to participate."

Brenner says his personal mission is to grow SAP's culture of information participation. With sixty thousand employees, the company currently has approximately fifty intermittent contributors, and just two routine evangelists. But, at present, with a wholly volunteer participation framework and an internal culture that hasn't historically embraced insourcing, it's tough sledding. "We need to cross the line from enablement to encouragement," he says.

Considering the *SAP Business Innovation* blog (ar.gy/sapinnovation) is already a success, even with sparse participation, additional participation could grow results geometrically. The site already generates thousands of visits per day, and the conversion rate—measured by the percentage of people who go from the blog to the main SAP site and fill out a contact form in exchange for an information download—is higher than for visitors coming to the main site directly.

Brenner believes that smaller companies have an easier time with insourcing because cultural shifts are quicker to take root, and employees have a better, organic sense of who has what expertise. Even though it's a big change for a large, global company, Brenner says it's a requirement. "It's the content we produce that is going to help us engage with new customers, that is going to help us grow new business. You need to get every employee on that bandwagon."

IBM and Assisted Insourcing

Michael Brenner yearns to cross the line between enablement and encouragement. IBM has stepped fully across that line and now has thousands of employees as certified and active participants in social media and content creation.

IBM has adopted the Spark methodology, created by Massachusetts-based agency Digital Influence Group, which asks employees to use an interactive assessment tool that determines how they best fit into the insourcing framework at the company. Based on their current social involvement—for personal purposes or otherwise—and their answers to several questions about how and why they want to participate, the Spark system classifies employees by their proclivity to be effective in one or more of eight categories: Creator, Distributor, Solicitor, Responder, Listener, Conversationalist, Nurturer, Promoter.

The IBM version, called the Social Eminence Program, bridges social profiling (like the Myers-Briggs and similar tests) and behavior analysis to identify and leverage the point where employee behavioral preferences and brand objectives intersect. This is a critical success element of big insourcing efforts, as, with few exceptions (like the one profiled below), content creation and social participation typically fails when done via mandate or at the point of a bayonet. Enabling team members to help customers and prospects in the form and fashion they are most comfortable yields better outcomes, too.

IBM has a widely dispersed group of more than four thousand participants in the Social Eminence Program. They are cajoled and supported by Social Business managers who oversee all aspects of a social business program, acting as the personal conduit, coach, and trainer for the insourced participants, each of whom has a personal action plan tailored to their needs and wants. This personal approach matters. IBM found that employees trained as a group are "successful" at a ratio of approximately one in eleven, whereas employees trained and activated with individualized success plans succeed at a ratio of three in four (ar.gy/IBMinfluence).

OpenView Venture Partners and Mandatory Insourcing

It may be rare (today), but there are organizations where becoming a resource for customers and prospective customers in social media and beyond isn't a pilot project, a program, or an initiative. It's just the way business is done. Welcome to OpenView Venture Partners, where Youtility is omnipresent.

A thirty-person venture capital fund in Boston, OpenView goes to almost unfathomable lengths to provide a flood of massively useful information to their current portfolio of twenty expansion-stage technology companies, as well as to the next generation of prospective investment options that also consume the information created by OpenView (openviewpartners.com).

Every person at the company helps make and distribute useful information. It's part of their job description, and partially determines their compensation. And with thirty people helping, there's a lot of information coming out of OpenView. There is at least one article and one video per day, augmented by a weekly podcast, e-mail newsletter, and an interview with a business or marketing expert. Every quarter the company produces two e-books, two case studies, two reports, an infographic, and an online assessment tool. So sweeping is the commitment to information at OpenView that they built an in-house audio and video studio.

Especially in the context of cultural shifts mentioned by Michael Brenner of SAP and Tim Kopp from ExactTarget, it's interesting to note that OpenView didn't start out like this, but evolved over time. "Our founder Scott Maxwell read Joe Pulizzi's book *Get Content, Get Customers* and started drinking the Kool-Aid pretty quickly," says Kevin Cain, director of Content Strategy at OpenView. "He reached out to Joe, and they developed a relationship. Scott then brought it to OpenView and held a firm-wide meeting and started telling people that this is going to become part of our DNA."[4]

And so it has. Even though the Youtility is centered around OpenView's existing portfolio companies and answering the questions about growth and business success they have, the ultimate audience is, of course, much larger. The company's various websites and blogs generate forty-five thousand visitors each month, and OpenView believes all that information differentiates them in a very crowded venture capital marketplace.

"Three or four years ago when we were getting started, our outbound team—the folks that call out to all the companies we might want to invest in—were doing tons of calls every week," says Cain. "Eight out of ten times, they'd pick up the phone and the person at the other end had no idea who OpenView was. It just was not a name on their radar. Today, nine out of ten know who we are, and a lot of that is because of the content."

OpenView is proving that mandatory insourcing can work—if it's woven into the fabric of the organization.

CHAPTER 11
Make Youtility a Process, Not a Project

I hope you are compelled after reading this book to launch an initiative to create inherently useful marketing, to use friend-of-mine awareness to differentiate your company, and to break through the invitation avalanche. But do not assign a completion date, because Youtility is never finished.

Indeed you can embrace the principles in these pages and become useful, but that usefulness is temporal and fleeting. As soon as you've successfully answered the questions and provided the information needed by customers and prospects, it's time to determine how you can be even more helpful the next time. Youtility is not a project with a beginning, a middle, and an end. Rather it requires an ongoing, never-ending, constantly reinvented and refined process.

"The first thing I tell anybody; any client I'm working with who wants to focus on this stuff, I explain to them, 'This is not a short-term play. It requires a long-term, ongoing initiative to be done right," says C. C. Chapman. "You have to be constantly thinking, 'Okay, well what are we going to do next? What are we going to do down the road?'"[1]

At interactive marketing firm Ethology, this type of ongoing content creation and information provision isn't an adjunct to other disciplines like e-mail marketing, search engine optimization, and online advertising. Instead, it's at the center of the firm's recommendations to corporate clients. Even though specific elements of Youtility can be successfully tackled over a concise time horizon, there is no finish line for the effort as a whole.

"In our opinion this never ends because you're not going to hit a grand slam every time, right?" asks Mike Corak, executive vice president at Ethology. "We've got to figure out what's really going to resonate long term and provide more of that through different channels. We really think that this is an ongoing process, and a job that needs to be thought about as part of the core marketing and advertising mix now."[2]

There are three reasons why successes in this area can be fleeting, and why your efforts must be sustained once you commence: Customer needs change, technology shifts, and new ideas are conceived.

Your Customers May Need Something Different from You Tomorrow

It's terrific and commendable if you've used data and research to effectively understand customer needs and map them to useful marketing programs, like the companies profiled in this book. But, invariably, those customer needs will eventually change, and the pace of innovation and the real-time nature of information dissemination dictate that change will occur faster than ever.

Clorox encountered this with their myStain app. According to David Kellis, "One of the things that we've learned about building an app that we didn't realize when we started it is that the startup cost is fairly low, but you can't just build something and then leave it there, right? So we've had to build a budget every year to do updates of the app, and most of the updates were adding new stains or adding seasonal-type stains. So holiday stains, like cranberry sauce in the winter and popcorn in the summer, or things you would eat at a July Fourth barbecue."[3]

Speaking of barbecue, Sterling Ball from Big Poppa Smokers and PelletSmoking.com recently expanded his information empire into another new corner of that subculture, launching DrumSmoking.com as a parallel discussion forum and advice portal for enthusiasts of drum smokers (created when you cut up a fifty-five gallon drum and make an ersatz smoker out of it). Shrewdly, Ball sells conversion kits and parts.

One industry where customer needs change with remarkable rapidity is in Greg Ng's world of frozen food. When asked whether he's ever considered reviewing other types of products, he acknowledges pondering the option but recognizes he'll never, ever be finished with his core concept. "The brand Lean Cuisine alone, for example, at one point was releasing 150 different frozen offerings every quarter. So it's going to take a while for me to blow through that," Ng says. "Some of those stay on the roster quarter by quarter, but at any given time they have over 100 different offerings in the freezer aisle. And that's just one brand."[4]

New restaurants open in Banff that Taxi Mike has to categorize. Meijer stocks new products that have to be GPS mapped in the Find-It application. At this point there may not be a wide array of new knots being developed for Columbia to incorporate in future editions of their app, but perhaps their research will determine that customers now need lantern advice, or counsel on best food options to bring along on an outdoor adventure. (I smell an opportunity for a Columbia partnership with Greg Ng and *Freezer Burns*.) Your customers' needs will change, too, and you must be prepared to react, update, and expand accordingly—before a competitor does.

New Technology Opens the Door to Youtility Variations

Several of the companies profiled in this book have chosen mobile applications as a primary way to manifest their usefulness. This is, of course, one example of how technology shifts require you to treat these efforts as a process, not a project. Angie's List has lived through several shifts of this type, going from a small, neighborhood directory to a telephone service to a full-featured website and mobile application. Here's one of my favorite instances of technology altering the format of Youtility and providing newfound depth and relevance.

Cloth is a mobile application that makes it easy to save, categorize, and share your favorite outfits. Developed in December 2011 by Wray Serna and her boyfriend, Seth Porges, a former editor at *Maxim* and *Popular Mechanics*, the genesis of the idea came from Serna's habit of taking pictures of herself wearing outfits she planned to pack on trips.

"I asked, 'Wray, what are you doing?'" recalls Porges. "She said, 'Whenever I have an outfit I like, I take a picture of it and save it for later so I can remember it.' I realized that people have hundreds of articles of clothing and ensembles and it all fits together like pieces in a jigsaw puzzle."[5]

Porges also recognized that the majority of the photographs people take of themselves wearing clothes are shot with a mobile device, creating a haphazard and chaotic storage system, with many of the photos never to be seen again.

"That's where Cloth came about," Porges says. "The idea of 'All right, how can we create the first utility that allows you to hold onto the photos of the outfits you like, and then do things with them once you have them?'"

This concept of Youtility, serving the needs of the clothing owner, are unusual in this category, according to Porges, who bemoans the litany of mobile applications and websites created by fashion brands and clothing retailers for the sole purpose of advertising and direct promotion.

My mom would absolutely love Cloth, and as soon as she buys a smartphone, I'm installing it. A former teacher, she's a clothes and shoes buff, who set out each school year to never wear the same outfit twice. She logged it all in a tiny notebook throughout the seventies, eighties, and nineties. I can hardly fathom the mindshare Cloth would have freed up for her.

The customer-centric nature of Cloth has served the company well, and it has received glowing press in the fashion and technology communities. Despite its initial success, Cloth wasn't finished. In June 2012, they launched a new version that incorporated a live feed from weather-data provider Wunderground. This allows the Cloth app to not only organize your outfits, but also recommend them based on real-time meteorological conditions and future weather forecasts. It's an entirely new layer of Youtility, enabled by the combination of two technologies. Being able to look at all of your "comfy" outfits on your phone and select one while still in bed (in theory), is interesting. Doing so and then having the app tell you to not wear a scarf because it's supposed to be 80 degrees is far more intriguing. There's nothing like being admonished by your mobile gadgets.

The Cloth app remains free, with the weather feature costing ninety-nine cents as an in-application upgrade. Users certainly don't seem to mind, as Cloth carries a 4.5 average rating (out of 5) in the Apple iTunes store. The company created an excellent overview video (ar.gy/cloth), explaining the new weather feature.

"Cloth is not done and probably never will be done," says Porges. "Technologies change, people change, users change, and you have to be there to adapt to it or else you will be making cassettes when the CD comes around."

Good Ideas Don't Have an Expiration Date

The third reason why Youtility must be a process, not a project, is that while good Youtility is better than no Youtility, great Youtility isn't easy. You can't schedule greatness, and it doesn't respond well to deadlines and ultimatums.

Greatness comes from perseverance, which takes time. And it comes from inspiration, which can come at any time, from anybody. By making helpful marketing a never-ending part of your company's cultural DNA, you enable greatness to emerge whenever and however it can. This is the spirit that fostered RunPee, perhaps the most useful application yet devised (for moviegoers, at least).

Dan Florio is a character. Formerly a programmer for Microsoft Xbox, he grew up in the historic mining town of Bisbee, Arizona, and went to college at Northern Arizona University in Flagstaff. He spent most of his freshman year money on a Dell laptop, and could only afford living in a tent near campus for a year. He made pocket money by modeling nude for the art department. He studied abroad in Wales and spent a few years working in math and astronomy at the University of Arizona (my alma mater). Oh, and he's a trained massage therapist. You want to have a beer with Dan Florio.

In 2005, while watching the more-than-three-hour, full-length, Peter Jackson–directed version of *King Kong* with his wife, Jill, Dan Florio mentioned aloud that it would be

MAKE YOUTILITY A PROCESS, NOT A PROJECT

great to have a website that listed the parts of a movie during
which you could use the restroom without missing any key
scenes. Research determined that such a site did not exist, so
he built RunPee.com, where you can determine with second-
by-second precision when are the best times to dash out to
the bathroom during a movie. The site's tagline is: "Because
Movie Theaters Don't Have Pause Buttons."

The site, organized by movie title and release date, provides a helpful synopsis of the first five minutes of the film
(if you're running late). But the recommendations for "run
pee" windows are the most useful feature. For example, in
the movie *Life of Pi*, he suggests potential breaks at fifty-five
minutes into the movie (a four-minute opportunity), at one
hour, four minutes into the movie (for five minutes), and at
one hour, twenty-one minutes (for three minutes). For each
window, he provides a dialog cue, alerting you that it's time
to go. The mobile application on iOS, Android, and Windows phones is even better because you press one button
when the film begins, and, when an opportunity occurs, your
phone vibrates to let you know how much time you have.
When you return, the website or mobile app provides a sur-
prisingly detailed synopsis of what you've missed. RunPee
also tells you if anything happens after the credits, as more
and more filmmakers are using that time as a creative ap-
pendix or afterword. It's an app that is most definitely worth
ninety-nine cents.

RunPee is a family affair. Dan Florio, his mother, and his
sister still see and review every movie. Determining the "pee
times," as he calls them, isn't as easy as you might think:

"We have to sit in the movie theater and take notes. It
tends to be hard to do pee times for character-driven movies
because every scene is important to the development of the

character. Whereas, in an action movie, there's a car chase scene and that's a pee time because, well, there's five other car chase scenes that are better than this one."[6]

Being able to make a living reviewing movies in this strange way is certainly gratifying to Florio, who says on an average day RunPee generates 250 new downloads. But the application also genuinely improves the lives of some people. "For some people, it's really nice knowing if anything happens after the credits. That's all they use it for, and it's not a huge deal," Florio says. "But for other people, who love going to the movies but have renal issues or are pregnant and cannot sit through a movie without needing to pee, this profoundly impacts their movie-going experience." The app is so popular among expecting mothers that it's been covered by *Pregnancy* magazine.

"It works because it is a nice utility," says Florio. "And I've never spent a dime on marketing. It's just an easy story to tell. People tell their friends, 'I've got to tell you about this app, it's the coolest thing.' And it's not the coolest thing. It's a novelty. But it's a novelty with utility."

You got that right, Mr. Florio.

CHAPTER 12
Keeping Score

I f Youtility is going to be more than a marginalized novelty for you and your company, it must be measured effectively. As described by executives in interviews throughout this book, shifting from legacy, top-of-mind awareness, and interruption marketing to providing truly useful information is a big shift. It may not happen immediately, and I can almost guarantee that it won't happen easily. There are two ways to convince those skeptical about the power of Youtility.

First, ask them to think about how companies are being forced to compete for attention with people, and then to consider how much more they personally rely on helpful information provided by businesses. Blogs, mobile apps, helpful videos, free webinars, brand-published magazines—all of these are information sources that doubters in your company may be happily digesting without understanding that their provision is part of the umbrella strategy of Youtility.

Second, prove your point with numbers, but make sure you attempt to do so with numbers that matter. Remember, the objective is not just to create Youtility for the sake of it, but to improve your business in the process. Consequently, you need to measure the ways your efforts in this area are improving the business. Certainly there are instances, some profiled here, where providing truly useful information *is* the business, in its entirety. *Freezer Burns* fits into this category. So does Cloth and RunPee. But it's more likely that your usefulness will need to be tied to a desirable business outcome. Youtility isn't the end, but a means to an end for companies like River Pools, Clorox, Hilton Suggests, SAP, and many, many more.

The numbers that you use to determine effectiveness will vary somewhat based on company type, size, data availability, and the type of Youtility you're providing. Categorically, however, there are four distinct types of numbers used to measure the impact of this type of marketing: consumption metrics, advocacy and sharing metrics, lead-generating metrics, and sales metrics.

It's important to understand these four categories and to recognize that there are many specific measures available within each segment. To do this right and to do it well, you will need to track multiple data points. There is no "magic number" when measuring this type of marketing.

Consumption Metrics

These are the easiest to track because they are almost always available from within the platform where the Youtility exists. If you want to know how often your mobile app was downloaded (and you do if you have a mobile app), you can look at your app store publisher account and find out. If you want to know how many people are reading your blog or watching your video, that data is available within your blog software and video hosting system, respectively. Certainly, for any online, helpful marketing, you should be able to derive consumption metrics. It's less simple for offline iterations of Youtility; Taxi Mike may not have a precise mechanism for determining how many people use his Dining Guide, other than when he needs to print more. Same with Duracell showing up in New York City with a mobile phone–charging unit after Superstorm Sandy. Representatives manning the truck could log usage by hand, and that may be the only logical way to gauge consumption in a circumstance like that.

A note of caution: Many companies measure only consumption metrics, which is a failure of math, and of imagination. Think about the *SAP Business Innovation* blog. If Michael Brenner and his team there only tracked consumption, they would look only at how many people visited the blog; and while that tells a story of success, it doesn't tell the real story. Remember that the strategic thrust for that program was to get SAP involved in conversations about topics other than SAP and the areas they already dominate. So, Michael measures precisely which search terms bring visitors to the blog, to be able to measure whether they are, in fact, getting involved in those areas. But even that doesn't go deep enough.

Yes, this type of marketing dictates that every company become a publishing company at some level. It doesn't mean, however, that you adopt the publishing business

model, whereby eyeballs are translated into revenue in a linear way. Greg Ng from *Freezer Burns* can do that because
the more people who watch his videos, the more advertising revenue he generates. But that's very much an exception.
Creating more visitors to your website, for example, should
spur questions along with congratulations: Do people reading the *SAP Business Innovation* blog engage in other, more
desirable behaviors on the website? Do people who read the
blog subsequently sign up for an e-mail newsletter? Do they
come back to the site over and over, or just once? And if
they do come back, is it at a ratio that's better than website
visitors overall?

Brenner and SAP are tracking all of this, and more. They
aren't interested in eyeballs per se; they are interested in the
behaviors those eyeballs engage in, and you should be as well.

Advocacy and Sharing Metrics

Sharing metrics—measurements of how often your helpful
information is forwarded to a friend, tweeted, shared on
Facebook, or other behaviors of similar type and circumstance—are another straightforward way to quantify online
information. Also within this category are reviews, which
are particularly important for mobile applications. In almost
every case, the platform you utilize will either count sharing and reviews natively, or you'll easily be able to calculate
them yourself.

McDonald's Canada closely studies how many people
subscribe to "watch" a question, the feature that posts an
eventual answer to the subscriber's Facebook page for all of
their friends to see. This is an excellent example of an advo-

cacy and sharing metric. One of the reasons the program is considered such a huge success: 19,000 questions asked is one thing; 6.5 million questions read is a different magnitude of remarkable.

Holiday World can track how many people comment on their YouTube videos of each ride and how many people "like" each ride on Facebook. Scott's Miracle-Gro tracks how often their useful e-mails are forwarded to other people by e-mail subscribers.

Note though that sharing and advocacy metrics are overvalued in most organizations, because they are public and personal. We care too much about Facebook "likes," tweets, shares, and such because no report or analysis needs to be conducted. The numbers are just sitting there, staring us in the face and begging us to measure up versus competitors. Reviews are almost insidious in their psychological impact. A mobile application might have three hundred thousand downloads but only ninety reviews. Eighty of them could be positive, but the ten that are not carry significant force in many companies. It's okay to be responsive to bad reviews—you should be—but don't let the tail wag the dog mathematically.

Lead-Generation Metrics

These are numbers that indicate that someone consuming your helpful marketing is considering a purchase, or at least wants to learn more, or hopes to interact with your company in a more reliable fashion. This is where you corral the hand raisers, and where interest starts to translate into revenue-generating action. Each time somebody uses the Syncapse

Facebook Advertising Budget calculator, it creates a lead for the company. Those people can then be contacted by Syncapse with offers for additional, customized assistance. Business-to-business companies like Syncapse often have an easier time calculating lead-generation metrics because those prospective customers have been conditioned over time—at least online—to provide personal information to download or access valuable information. It's a quid pro quo. They give you their name so you can follow up with them, and you give them Youtility. Remember, though, that a major driver of this entire trend is that Internet access has made us massively passive-aggressive, and reluctant to engage in this data exchange. Many of your prospective customers will be learning all about you from your own information and elsewhere, and you'll never even know it. This is what Brian Halligan from HubSpot was referencing when he emphasized in chapter 3 how critical it is for companies to provide self-serve information at the top of the consideration funnel. That's why several companies—even in business to business where lead-generation is engaged in with messianic zeal—are experimenting with doing away altogether with requiring prospects to fill out forms.

"Forms are the enemy of spread," says Joe Chernov of Kinvey, who believes if the Youtility is strong enough, prospects will contact the company unilaterally after they've finished their research.[1]

This is approximately how Marcus Sheridan of River Pools and Spas handles their helpful information. No exchange of data is required for prospective swimming pool buyers to read the more than 850 blog posts offered online. Once those prospects are sufficiently informed and educated, they make the first move.

Sales Metrics

If you're selling online or have an integrated database, determining the exact revenue impact of your helpful marketing is entirely viable. River Pools and Spas knows precisely what the revenue value of their overall program is because they know which customers came from the blog, and what each subsequent swimming pool installation generated for the company financially. In fact, the HubSpot software River Pools and Spas uses to manage their blog shows what the revenue contribution is for every specific article, so Sheridan and his team know which topics are driving leads and sales and which are not. In 2012 Google launched a similar metric in their Google Analytics software. Called "page value," it allows website owners to determine the impact of individual pages on lead generation and sales.

Warby Parker can track whether the people whose questions they've answered online have subsequently purchased glasses from the company, and whether the ratio of inquiry to purchase is higher than usual. They can also determine if people helped with custom videos tend toward higher-than-average order sizes or more frequent ordering. When you buy barbecue equipment or supplies from him online, Sterling Ball at Big Poppa Smokers most definitely knows if you're also a frequent contributor to the PelletSmoking.com forums.

If you're not selling online, or if your Youtility efforts extend to multiple platforms, tracking the immediate sales impact is more difficult, but it's possible. Meijer, for instance, has coupons and offers included in their FindIt application. So, while it's not possible today to determine the full financial impact of being able to locate items in Meijer stores more quickly, they can track offer redemptions from within the application.

Could Columbia Sportswear determine whether people who download the knots application subsequently purchase outdoor gear on their website? Conceivably, yes. But considering that Columbia products are also sold in many retail stores around the world, the metrics trail grows cold eventually. Learn what's possible and feasible in your own organization in terms of tracking sales from Youtility.

Return on Investment: Is This Worth the Effort?

Youtility isn't inexpensive; it's just a different type of expensive. With the exception of costs associated with marketing your marketing, creating useful marketing isn't a venture that requires substantial financial investments. Instead, the costs accrue in time and effort. This is a never-ending process, not a project that gets done and then paid for like a television commercial.

The type of program you adopt, and how clearly you can measure lead-generating and sales metrics within it, will dictate your ability to determine the finite return on investment (ROI) of your Youtility program. Assuming a best-case scenario for illustration purposes, let's consider the ROI of a robust, informative blog effort like River Pools and Spas. Note that these are not actual numbers for River Pools, but an example of how you would make this calculation.

Let's say it takes an average of forty hours per month to produce the blog. Let's also say that the average hourly compensation of people working on the blog in the company is

$40 per hour ($80,000 per year, divided by two thousand work hours—the standard formula in the United States). Let's further stipulate that the overhead factor for the company is 50 percent. This figures in benefits, marketing, taxes, and other costs. If you don't know the standard overhead factor for your company, ask an accounting manager or owner. Let's also figure that your blog cost $12,000 to design and produce, and that you plan to redesign it annually. You can amortize that as a $1,000 per month fee. Also add in $100 per month in blog hosting fees to maintain the website, and $100 per month in miscellaneous expenses.

It adds up like this:

Labor (40 hours × $40 × 0.50 overhead)	$2,400 per month
Design	$1,000 per month
Hosting	$ 100 per month
Miscellaneous	$ 100 per month
Total blog investment	$3,600 per month

Now the revenue side. Let's say you generate twenty-five leads per month from prospective customers filling out an interest form on the blog, or calling a special, trackable phone number that you only show on the pages of the blog. Let's say 20 percent of those leads become customers, which is an aggressive estimate, but join me in believing that you're disproportionately good at this. Let's further project that the typical lifetime value of your customers—the amount they spend with you on average, ever—is $3,000 each. Finally, let's assume your operating margin on the products or services you provide is 30 percent, meaning that your profit on that $3,000 lifetime spend is $900.

It adds up like this:

Leads from blog	25 per month
Conversion rate (leads to sales)	20 percent
Total sales from blog	5 per month
Average lifetime value, per customer	$3,000
Operating margin	30 percent
Average lifetime profit, per customer	$900
Average lifetime profit from blog	$4,500 per month

Calculating ROI is simple and straightforward. It is always the same, as it's a standard formula not subject to interpretation or conjecture. ROI is always return minus investment, divided by investment, then expressed as a percentage.

In our example then, it would look like this:

($4,500 – $3,600)/$3,600 = 25 percent

The return on investment for this hypothetical blog is 25 percent, and you can use the same analysis and evaluation methodology for each component of your Youtility program.

Sometimes, however, you cannot track ROI cleanly, and in those instances you may want to fall back on correlation as a way to assess overall value. In a correlation system, you create one unified spreadsheet and you plot, over a period of months, everything that happened to your company that might impact marketing success. Track consumption metrics, and sharing metrics, and public relations mentions, and new top-of-mind awareness campaigns, website traffic, and more. Then, track lead-generation metrics, if you can get them, and overall, company-wide sales metrics like total revenue, new customers, and average order size. Add the lead generation and sales data to the spreadsheet calendar containing your marketing activities and results. What you're looking for are correlated spikes in success. When mobile downloads went up, shortly thereafter new customers went up, too, even though nothing else had changed in the marketing mix. Does this prove that your mobile application was responsible for an increase in sales? It does not. But, if you continue to see correlated trends like that, you can be reasonably confident that some relationship exists, and you can then engage in more rigorous studies to disprove or prove that tie.

These types of correlation studies can require you to analyze results over a long period of time, looking for trends to emerge. This, however, fits neatly into the long-term nature of winning the war of information in general. Youtility is a marathon, not a sprint.

Freezer Burns' Ng epitomizes this philosophy. "My return my first year was twenty-three cents an hour. But that wasn't my goal," says Ng. "My goal for year one was to own the niche, was to put out so much content that even if someone had a bigger budget than I did, or more free time, that they would not want to get into my space."[2]

Each year brings new goals for Ng. "Year two was 'How do I grow my audience?' It wasn't really until the end of year two when I was like, 'You know what? Let's start monetizing,'" he recalls.

That doesn't mean it will, or should, take you multiple years to start seeing a return on your useful marketing, but recognize that you are planting seeds that will bloom in time, not necessarily overnight.

"The @HiltonSuggests program has almost zero immediate value to the company," says Vanessa Sain-Dieguez of
Hilton Worldwide. "But we've definitely seen that our interactions can result in bookings. If one day there are Hilton
Suggests in every single market, there is no price tag you can
put on that."[3]

Youtility: An Easy Reference Guide

If you've just finished reading the book, congratulations. You're well on your way to creating Youtility for your customers and prospects. I've provided this Easy Reference Guide so that you can quickly refresh your understanding of the key principles when needed. If you're the kind of person who flips to the back of the book right away, this Easy Reference Guide will give you an idea of what's included.

Introduction

KEY POINTS:

- If you sell something, you make a customer today. If you help someone, you may create a customer for life.

- There are two ways for companies to succeed in this era: be "amazing" or be useful. The latter is much reliable and viable.

- Youtility is marketing so useful, people would gladly pay for it.

Part I: Turning Marketing Upside Down

Chapter 1: Top-of-Mind Awareness

KEY POINTS:

- As a marketing strategy, top-of-mind awareness is less effective than ever:

- The media landscape is highly fractured.

- Companies are fundamentally distrusted by consumers.

- Trust has a huge impact on marketing success.

KEY DATA:

- Businesses are only trusted by 58 percent of global consumers.

- When a company is distrusted, 57 percent of people will believe negative information about it after hearing it just one or two times.

Chapter 2: Frame-of-Mind Awareness

KEY POINTS:

- Being found doesn't create demand, it can only fulfill it.

- Search engines' role in the website discovery funnel is weakening.

KEY DATA:

- Search engines were used by 83 percent of consumers to find websites pre-purchase in 2004. In 2012, it has 61 percent

- More than 30 percent of American social media users say social media has driven them to make a purchase.

Chapter 3: Friend-of-Mine Awareness

KEY POINTS:

- Today, companies must compete for attention against consumers' friends and family members.

- If your company and its marketing are truly, inherently useful, your customers and prospective customers will keep you close, as they keep their friends and family members close.

- Making your company useful without expectation of an immediate return is in direct opposition to the long-standing principles of successful marketing, and that's a good thing.

Part II: The Three Facets of Youtility

Chapter 4: Self-Serve Information

KEY POINTS:

- We've always tried to build loyalty with people, and now we must build loyalty with information.

- If your company isn't trying to win the zero moment of truth, you're losing customers you didn't even know you had a chance to get.

• • •

- Always-on Internet access has made us all passive-aggressive.

- Death of the salesmen: we now talk to a real person as a last resort, not as a first step.

KEY DATA:

- In 2010, shoppers needed 5.3 sources of information before making a purchase decision. In 2011, shoppers needed 10.4 pieces of information before making a purchase decision.

- From 2009 to 2011, American females' use of voice minutes on mobile phones decreased by 12 percent. During the same period their text messages sent and received increased by 35 percent.

- In B2B, customers will contact a sales rep only after independently completing 60 percent of the purchasing-decision process.

Chapter 5: Radical Transparency

KEY POINTS:

- Creating customers by answering their questions is imminently viable and carries remarkable, persuasive power.

- Unless it inhibits ease-of-use, there is no downside to providing extraordinarily detailed information to your prospective customers.

- It doesn't matter whether anyone in your industry is providing self-serve information—big companies are, and they're training all consumers to expect it.

KEY DATA:

- Companies with websites with 101 to 200 pages generate two-and-a-half times more leads than companies with 50 or fewer pages.

- Companies that blog fifteen or more times per month get five times more traffic than those that don't blog.

Chapter 6: Real-Time Relevancy

KEY POINTS:

- Youtility is real-time relationship building. You're either sufficiently useful at any given moment, and thus can connect with the customer, or you're not.

- For decades, the key question has been "how valuable is the brand?" The key question moving forward is "how valuable are your apps?"

- Within a generation every customer in every developed nation will have never known a world without the ability to access information at any time through a mobile device.

KEY DATA:

- By 2014 there will be more mobile Internet users than desktop Internet users.

- Forty-five percent of American social media users research products or brands on a smartphone multiple times per week.

- There are 2.9 billion mobile subscriptions in Asia and the Pacific, compared to 969 million in the Americas.

Part III: Six Blueprints to Create Youtility

Chapter 7: Identify Customer Needs

KEY POINTS:

- You have to understand what your prospective customers need to make better decisions, and how you can improve their lives by providing it.

- Search engines, social chatter, and web analytics data will help you understand customer needs.

- The best way to understand customer needs is to ask real customers.

Chapter 8: Map Customer Needs to Useful Marketing

KEY POINTS:

- Determining which is the optimal conveyance for Youtility requires a level of research beyond understanding customer needs.

- You have to understand not just what your customers need, but how and where they prefer to access information.

- Atomize your marketing to reach a larger audience.

Chapter 9: Market Your Marketing

KEY POINTS:

- People are not going to magically find your Youtility, you have to add promotional support.

- Content is fire, and social media is gasoline.

- Use social media to promote your useful information first, and your company second.

- Your employees are your most important—and most overlooked—audience.

Chapter 10: Insource Youtility

KEY POINTS:

- Everything important in business starts as a job, and eventually becomes a skill.

- Being useful must be part of your company DNA.

- Involving a wide variety of employees not only makes it easier to create and maintain helpful information, it also increases effectiveness because they bring credibility that centralized, official communication doesn't have.

- There are four types of Youtility insourcing:
  - Circumstantial insourcing
  - Voluntary insourcing
  - Assisted insourcing
  - Mandatory insourcing

KEY DATA:

- Company experts are trusted by 66 percent of people; regular employees are trusted by 50 percent; and CEOs are trusted by 38 percent.

• • •

Chapter 11: Make Youtility a Process, Not a Project

KEY POINTS:

- Youtility requires a never-ending, constantly reinvented and refined process.

- There are three reasons this must be a ongoing program:
  - Customer needs change;
  - Technology shifts;
  - New and better ideas are conceived.

- You can't schedule greatness, and it doesn't respond well to deadlines and ultimatums.

Chapter 12: Keeping Score

KEY POINTS:

- If Youtility is going to be more than a marginalized novelty for you and your company, it must be measured effectively.

- There are four categories of measurement that matter:
  - Consumption metrics
  - Advocacy and Sharing metrics
  - Lead-generation metrics
  - Sales metrics

- Return on Investment is absolutely calculable for many types of Youtility. Where it isn't, consider correlation analysis.

ACKNOWLEDGMENTS

Thank you to my wife, Alyson, and my children, Annika and Ethan, from whom I stole time and attention to work on this. I love you. Thank you also to my amazing team at Convince & Convert for keeping fingers in the dike while I created this book.

Speaking of Convince & Convert, a huge debt of gratitude to readers of my blog, subscribers to my e-mails, listeners to my podcast, and attendees at my speeches. Without your support, none of this happens.

Extra special thanks to Kim Corak, whose help with the research and interviews made this project possible, and to the dozens of marketing professionals we talked to, who, every day, are effectively using the principles in this book.

Many thanks to my old friend Michael Hale, whose hand-drawn interpretations of charts and graphs decorate these pages.

Thank you to Tamsen Webster for her sound editorial direction and advice; and to Marcus Sheridan for his inspiration and for the wonderful foreword he wrote for the book.

I very much appreciate the outstanding team at Portfolio (especially my thoughtful and patient editor Brooke Carey) for believing in me and *Youtility*, my publicists at

Fortier PR, and my agent Jim Levine for making it all come together.

And most of all, thank you to my mom, Joyce Hollis, who taught me how to write (among other things), and handled initial copyediting for this and my previous book.

AUTHOR'S NOTE: E-MAIL ME

I wrote this book as a reaction to the landslide of punditry that prescribes "make your company amazing" as a strategic approach. The reality is, your business probably isn't amazing, and you probably won't have the opportunity or time to make it so.

For my money—and yours—I vastly prefer to adopt a more defensible plan that will win hearts, minds, fans, and customers in a more viable and repeatable way. That plan is Youtility. If you create marketing that people genuinely want, you can dispense with the "shock," "awe," and "viral" and focus on solving problems, answering questions, and creating long-lasting customer relationships by doing so.

Your company is being forced to compete for your customers' attention against those customers' family members and best friends. If you're useful enough, and if you commit to inform rather than promote, customers will reward you with trust and loyalty.

The difference between helping and selling is just two letters. But those letters make all the difference.

• • •

| 198 | Continue the Conversation and Win Prizes at YoutilityBook.com

This isn't the end of Youtility, it's just the beginning. This trend, and the themes and principles it encompasses, will continue to grow and expand. I'll be chronicling success stories and best practices at the official website (youtilitybook.com), where you'll find resources to help you on your journey toward inherently useful marketing. I invite you to visit right now and see what's available.

Photo Contest

Take a photo of the book "In the Wild" and post it to Twitter or Instagram with the hashtag #Youtility, and you could win terrific, useful prizes and unlock bonus content. Details at youtilitybook.com.

Youtility in Your Company

And if you're interested in thinking through how you can apply the Youtility blueprints in your own company, through my consulting firm Convince & Convert, I conduct Youtility audits and work with people like you to create truly, inherently useful marketing.

Youtility Live

Lastly, if you think your company and/or your customers would be inspired by the Youtility message, let me know. I'm on the road often, addressing corporate and conference

audiences, showing people how smart marketing is about
help not hype.

I sincerely hope you enjoyed this book. But most of all, I
hope you found it useful. Because as you know now, that's
what it's all about.

I'd love to talk about the book, answer questions, and stay
connected. E-mail me at jay@convinceandconvert.com.

NOTES

Introduction

1. Boyle, Matthew, "Best Buy's Giant Gamble," *CNNMoney*, March 29, 2006, accessed January 21, 2013. http://money.cnn. com/magazines/fortune/fortune_archive/2006/04/03/8373034/ index.htm.

Chapter 1: Top-of-Mind Awareness

1. Interview with the author, October 11, 2012.
2. *Wikipedia* entry for top-rated programs, according to Nielsen ratings, accessed January 26, 2013. http://en.wikipedia.org/ wiki/Nielsen_ratings#Top-rated_programs.
3. Rick Edmonds et al., "Newspapers: By the Numbers," *The State of the News Media 2012*, accessed January 21, 2013. http://stateofthemedia.org/2012/newspapers-building-digital-revenues-proves-painfully-slow/newspapers-by-the-numbers.
4. Baer, Jay, "9 Surprising New Facts About Social Media in America," *Convince & Convert*, December 30, 2011, accessed January 21, 2013. http://www.convinceandconvert.com/social-media-strategy/9-surprising-new-facts-about-social-media-in-america-2.
5. "Buzz in the Blogosphere: Millions More Bloggers and Blog Readers," The Nielsen Company, accessed January 21, 2013.

http://blog.nielsen.com/nielsenwire/online_mobile/buzz-in-the-blogosphere-millions-more-bloggers-and-blog-readers.

6. Rohrs, Jeff and Stewart, Morgan, "The Social Break-Up," ExactTarget, downloaded January 21, 2013. http://www.exacttarget.com/subscribers-fans-followers/social-breakup.aspx.

7. Rohrs, Jeff and Stewart, Morgan, "The Social Break-Up UK," ExactTarget, downloaded January 21, 2013. http://www.exacttarget.com/subscribers-fans-followers/sff12.aspx.

8. "2013 Edelman Trust Barometer Executive Summary," Edelman, accessed January 26, 2013. http://scribd.com/doc/121501475/Exective-Summary-2013-Edelman-Trust-Barometer.

9. Interview with the author, October 11, 2012.

Chapter 2: Frame-of-Mind Awareness

1. Clark, Nick, "R for Recovery Plan? Yell Plots Digital Future," *The Independent,* May 18, 2011, accessed January 21, 2013. http://www.independent.co.uk/news/business/analysis-and-features/r-for-recovery-plan-yell-plots-digital-future-2285553.html.

2. Bellis, Mary, "The History of the Yellow Pages," *About.com,* accessed January 21, 2013. http://inventors.about.com/od/xyzstartinventions/a/yellow_pages.htm.

3. Wall, Aaron, "History of Search Engines: From 1945 to Google Today," *Search Engine History,* accessed January 21, 2013.

4. You just turned back to the author photo on the book jacket. Indeed, I look deceptively youthful. It's part of my charm.

5. Analysis of search volume for "inbound marketing" using Google Trends, Google, accessed January 21, 2013. http://www.google.com/trends/explore#q=inbound%20marketing.

6. Godin, Seth, "Harvest demand or create it?" *Seth Godin,* October 30, 2012, accessed January 21, 2013. http://sethgodin.typepad.com/seths_blog/2012/10/harvest-demand-or-create-it.html.

7. VanBoskirk, Shar, "The Forrester Wave: US Search Marketing Agencies, Q1 2011," Forrester, January 31, 2011, accessed January 21, 2013. http://www.icrossing.com/articles/forrester-search-wave-report-Q12011.pdf.

8. Ankeny, Jason, "Amazon acquires text-to-speech firm Ivona to rival Apple's Siri," *FierceMobile Content*, January 24, 2013, accessed January 26, 2013. http://www.fiercemobilecontent.com/story/amazon-acquires-text-speech-firm-ivona-rival-apples-siri/2013-01-24.

9. Tom Webster et al., "The Social Habit 2012 4Q Research Report," Edison Research, downloaded January 21, 2013. http://www.socialhabit.com.

10. Interview with the author, October 22, 2012.

11. Interview with the author, October 23, 2012.

12. Interview with the author, October 11, 2012.

Chapter 3: Friend-of-Mine Awareness

1. Webster et al., "The Social Habit . . ."

2. Interview with the author, September 7, 2012.

3. Interview with the author, September 18, 2012.

4. Interview with the author, September 14, 2012.

5. Interview with Kim Corak (of the Youtility research team), October 25, 2012.

6. 4 RUNNER, iTunes app store review of Sit or Squat, September 2, 2012, accessed January 21, 2013.

7. Interview with Kim Corak (of the Youtility research team), October 18, 2012.

8. Interview with the author, September 26, 2012.

9. Interview with the author, October 3, 2012.

Chapter 4: Self-Serve Information

1. Lecinski, Jim, "Winning the Zero Moment of Truth," Google, June 24, 2011, downloaded January 21, 2013. http://www.zeromomentoftruth.com.

2. Lecinski, "Winning the Zero Moment of Truth . . ."
3. Ibid.
4. Interview with the author, October 12, 2012.
5. Weidauer, Jeff, "Why Marketers Need to Rethink the Path to Purchase," *iMediaConnection*, April 3, 2012, accessed January 21, 2013. http://www.imediaconnection.com/content/31371.asp.
6. Solis, Brian, "Why Do Customers Use Social Networks for Customer Service? Because They Can . . ." *Brian Solis*, October 2, 2012, accessed January 21, 2013. http://www.briansolis. com/2012/10/why-do-customers-use-social-networks-for-customer-service-because-they-can.
7. Interview with the author, September 19, 2012.
8. Lapter, Ana, "The Most Important Number in B2B Marketing," *CEB Marketing*, August 31, 2011, accessed January 21, 2013. http://www.executiveboard.com/marketing-blog/the-most-important-number-in-b2b-marketing.
9. Lapter, "The Most Important Number in B2B Marketing . . ."
10. Interview with the author, September 26, 2012.
11. Brohan, Mark, "Sales Rise But Not Profits for Blue Nile in the Third Quarter," *Internet Retailer,* November 1, 2012, accessed January 21, 2013. http://www.internetretailer.com/2012/11/01/ sales-rise-not-profits-blue-nile-third-quarter.
12. "eBay Motors Fast Facts Q2 2012," eBay, accessed January 21, 2013. http://www.ebayinc.com/assets/pdf/fact_sheet/eBay_ Motors_Fact_Sheet_Q2_2012.pdf.
13. Baer, Jay, "Now THIS is How You Do Video Marketing as a Brand," *Convince & Convert*, December 20, 2011, accessed January 21, 2013. http://www.convinceandconvert.com/video-marketing/now-this-is-how-you-do-video-marketing-as-a-brand.
14. Interview with Kim Corak, of the Youtility research team, October 24, 2012.
15. "2012 Appy Awards Winners," MediaPost Communications, accessed January 21, 2013. http://www.mediapost.com/ appyawards/winners/?event=2012.

16. "An Interview with Big Poppa," *Hathway*, July 7, 2011, accessed January 21, 2013. http://www.wearehathway.com/ blog/web-development/an-interview-with-big-poppa.

17. "American Royal Grand Champion Winner Big Poppa Smokers," *Cowgirl's Country Life*, October 7, 2012, accessed January 21, 2013. http://cowgirlscountry.blogspot.com/2012/ 10/american-royal-grand-champion-winner.html.

18. Interview with Kim Corak, of the Youtility research team, October 23, 2012.

Chapter 5: Radical Transparency

1. Dan Koch and Paula Werne were interviewed by Kim Corak, of the Youtility research team, on October 2, 2012.

2. TripAdvisor reviews for Holiday World and Splashin' Safari on www.tripadvisor.com, accessed January 26, 2013.

3. Wroblewski, Luke, "The Continuing History of Amazon's Tab Navigation," *LukeW*, September 14, 2007, accessed January 26, 2013. http://lukew.com/ff/entry.asp?582.

4. Interview with the author, October 23, 2012.

5. Singel, Ryan, "Oct. 27, 1994: Web Gives Birth to Banner Ads," *Wired: This Day in Tech*, October 27, 2010, accessed January 26, 2013. http://www.wired.com/thisdayintech/2010/10/1027h otwired-banner-ads.

6. Interview with the author, October 23, 2012.

7. Interview with the author, September 26, 2012.

8. 1-800-BUTTERBALL or visit http://www.butterball.com/tips-how-tos/turkey-experts/overview.

9. Interview with the author, December 19, 2012.

10. Zax, David, "Fast Talk: How Warby Parker's Cofounders Disrupted the Eyewear Industry and Stayed Friends," *Fast Company*, February 22, 2012, accessed January 26, 2013. http:// www.fastcompany.com/1818215/fast-talk-how-warby-parkers-cofounders-disrupted-eyewear-industry-and-stayed-friends.

11. Interview with the author, September 26, 2012.

12. Greg still has his day job as an online marketer. *Freezer Burns* is strictly a hobby.

13. Interview with the author, November 7, 2012.

14. Rohrs, Jeff and Stewart, Morgan, "Retail Touchpoints Exposed," ExactTarget, downloaded January 26, 2013. http://assets.exacttarget.com/pdf/SFF16_WEB.pdf.

15. Interview with the author, September 14, 2012.

Chapter 6: Real-Time Relevancy

1. Colony, George, "The Mobile War," *Counterintuitive CEO*, October 15, 2012, accessed January 26, 2013. http://blogs.forrester.com/george_colony/12-10-15-the_mobile_war.

2. Paczkowski, John, "84 Million iPads, 400 Million iOS Devices and More Big Numbers From Apple," *All Things D*, September 12, 2012, accessed January 26, 2013. http://allthingsd.com/20120912/84-million-ipads-400-million-ios-devices-and-more-big-numbers-from-apple.

3. Lunden, Ingrid, "Free Apps Account for 89% Of All Downloads; Most Of The Rest Under $3; iOS Store Biggest Of Them All," *Techcrunch*, September 11, 2012, accessed January 26, 2013. http://Techcrunch.com/2012/09/11/free-apps.

4. "Global Mobile Statistics 2012 Part A: Mobile Subscribers; Handset Market Share; Mobile Operators," *mobiThinking*, December 2012, accessed January 26, 2013. http://mobithinking.com/mobile-marketing-tools/latest-mobile-stats/a#subscribers.

5. "What Makes Asia Pacific the Most Exciting Mobile Market in the World? Interview with Rohit Dadwal, MD Asia Pacific, MMA," *mobiThinking*, May 12, 2011, accessed January 26, 2013. http://mobithinking.com/mobile-asia-pacific-mma-interview.

6. Interview with the author, September 18, 2012.

7. Webster et al., "The Social Habit . . ."

8. "Factors Driving Millennial Shoppers' CPG Brand Selection," *Marketingcharts.com* via SymphonyIRI, July 2012, accessed

January 26, 2013. http://www.marketingcharts.com/direct/
millennials-cpg-brand-choices-influenced-by-promotions-new-
media-22573/symphonyiri-millennials-cpg-brand-decision-
factors-july2012png.
9. Interview with Kim Corak, of the Youtility research team,
October 18, 2012.
10. Brownell, Matt, "Can Retailers Beat the 'Showrooming' Effect
This Christmas?" *Daily Finance*, October 22, 2012, accessed
January 26, 2013. http://www.dailyfinance.com/2012/10/22/
christmas-shopping-showrooming-online-price-match.
11. Deckert, Steve, "Dear Best Buy, Target & Other Retailers:
Showrooming Isn't Your Problem," *Sweettooth*, September 17,
2012, accessed January 26, 2013. http://www
.sweettooth rewards.com/blog/2012/09/17/dear-best-buy-
target-other-retailers-showrooming-isnt-the-problem.
12. Kelly, Meghan, "Makeup retailer Sephora launches iPad
program (exclusive)," *Venture Beat,* March 13, 2012, accessed
January 26, 2013. http://venturebeat.com/2012/03/13/sephora-
apple-ipad.
13. Longoria, Diane, "Top 3 Retailers Defeating Showrooming,"
The Adventures of Pointman, November 8, 2012, accessed
January 26, 2013. http://www.pointsmith.com/blog/top-3-
retailers-defeating-showrooming.
14. Interview with the author, September 25, 2012.
15. Interview with the author, October 22, 2012.
16. Interview with the author, October 22, 2012.
17. Malik, Om, "New app MindMeld heralds the era of
anticipatory computing," *GIGAOM*, September 11, 2012,
accessed January 26, 2013. http://www.gigaom
.com/2012/09/11/new-app-mindmeld-heralds-the-era-of-
anticipatory-computing.
18. Galil, Leor, "Dan Deacon's App Can Help Create A New Concert
Experience," *Forbes.com*, August 31, 2012, accessed January
26, 2013. http://www.forbes.com/sites/leorgalil/2012/08/31/dan-
deacons-app-can-help-create-a-new-concert-experience.

19. Interview with Kim Corak, of the Youtility research team, October 12, 2012.
20. Interview with the author, November 23, 2012.
21. Interview with Kim Corak, of the Youtility research team, November 4, 2012.

Chapter 7: Identify Customer Needs

1. Interview with the author, September 19, 2012.
2. Search for "pellet smokers" on Google Trends (U.S. searches only), accessed November 24, 2012. http://www.google.com/trends/explore#q=pellet%20smokers&geo=US&cmpt=q.
3. Search for "Facebook advertising" on Google Keyword Tool, accessed November 24, 2012. https://adwords.google.com/o/Targeting/Explorer?__c=1000000000&__u=1000000000&ideaRequestType=KEYWORD_IDEAS.
4. The Big 12 is a conference of U.S. universities in the Midwest and Southwest.
5. Interview with the author, September 21, 2012.
6. "Long Tail" is derived from Chris Anderson's book of the same name, and is common interactive marketing parlance used to describe low-volume, highly specific search terms that are often used by consumers when they are deeper in the research process. "Sony television," vs. "Sony 50-inch LCD 3D television," for example.
7. Sentiment analysis shows how often the brand is mentioned in a positive versus negative context within social media.
8. Interview with the author, September 19, 2012.
9. Interview with the author, October 22, 2012.

Chapter 8: Map Customer Needs to Useful Marketing

1. Reviews of What Knot to Do in the Greater Outdoors app, Apple iTunes Store, accessed November 25, 2012.

2. Interview with Kim Corak, of the Youtility research team, November 19, 2012.

3. Interview with the author, October 5, 2012.

4. Interview with the author, September 24, 2012.

5. Neff, Jack, "Duracell Brings Charging Stations to Battery Park After Hurricane Sandy," *AdvertisingAge*, October 31, 2012, accessed January 26, 2013. http://adage.com/article/news/duracell-brings-charging-stations-battery-park/238078.

6. Interview with the author, September 24, 2012.

7. "Global Cloud Index (GCI)," Cisco, accessed January 26, 2013. http://www.cisco.com/en/US/netsol/ns1175/networking_solutions_sub_solution.html.

8. Interview with the author, September 24, 2012.

9. Interview with the author, October 9, 2012.

Chapter 9: Market Your Marketing

1. Interview with the author, October 11, 2012.

2. Interview with the author, September 18, 2012.

3. Interview with the author, October 3, 2012.

4. Rose, Robert, "Brand Storytelling Lessons from the Content 2020 Project," *Content Marketing Institute*, November 4, 2012, accessed January 26, 2013. http://contentmarketinginstitute.com/2012/11/brand-storytelling-content-2020-3.

5. Interview with Kim Corak, of the Youtility research team, October 23, 2012.

6. ExactTarget on Facebook and ExactTarget on Twitter, accessed December 1, 2012. http://www.facebook.com/exacttarget and http://www.twitter.com/exacttarget.

7. *Wikipedia* entry for ExactTarget, accessed January 26, 2013. http://en.wikipedia.org/wiki/ExactTarget.

8. Webster et al., "The Social Habit . . ."

9. "Facebook: A Profile of its 'Friends'," *Pew Internet Tumblr*, May 16, 2012, accessed January 26, 2013. http://pewresearch

.org/pubs/2262/facebook-ipo-friends-profile-social-networking-habits-privacy-online-behavior.

10. Roberts, Jeff John, "Typical Twitter User is a Young Woman with an iPhone & 208 Followers," *GIGAOM*, October 10, 2012, accessed January 26, 2013. http://gigaom.com/2012/10/10/the-typical-twitter-user-is-a-young-woman-with-an-iphone-and-208-followers/.

11. Interview with the author, October 3, 2012.

Chapter 10: Insource Youtility

1. Interview with the author, October 11, 2012.
2. Interview with the author, October 23, 2012.
3. Interview with the author, October 11, 2012.
4. Interview with the author, October 4, 2012.

Chapter 11: Make Youtility a Process, Not a Project

1. Interview with the author, October 3, 2012.
2. Interview with the author, September 21, 2012.
3. Interview with Kim Corak, of the Youtility research team, October 24, 2012.
4. Interview with the author, November 7, 2012.
5. Interview with Kim Corak, of the Youtility research team, October 23, 2012.
6. Interview with Kim Corak, of the Youtility research team, September 25, 2012.

Chapter 12: Keeping Score

1. Interview with the author, October 9, 2012.
2. Interview with the author, November 7, 2012.
3. Interview with the author, September 7, 2012.

INDEX